William Littleton Clark Hunnicutt

Prize-fighting in the Schools

And other Essays

William Littleton Clark Hunnicutt

Prize-fighting in the Schools
And other Essays

ISBN/EAN: 9783337233716

Printed in Europe, USA, Canada, Australia, Japan

Cover: Foto ©ninafisch / pixelio.de

More available books at **www.hansebooks.com**

PRIZE-FIGHTING IN THE SCHOOLS,

And Other Essays.

BY

W. L. C. HUNNICUTT, D.D.

Fitly to express a worthy thought is to give it wings and send it forth, preassured of welcome and appreciation in every mind.

NASHVILLE, TENN.:
PUBLISHING HOUSE M. E. CHURCH, SOUTH.
BARBEE & SMITH, AGENTS.
1898.

PREFACE.

In offering this book to the reading public the author hopes to help some, especially the young, to better thinking and wiser action in connection with the subjects herein discussed.

He does not claim to be a poet, but ventures to intersperse the essays with verses with a view to varying (he hopes not unpleasantly) the contents of the book.

He asks for the thoughts herein presented only that consideration which an earnest inquirer after truth should expect from those actuated by the same motive.

Believing that these essays will at least provoke, if they do not impart, some valuable thoughts on their several themes, the author sends them forth to the kindly reader. W. L. C. H.

Gloster, Miss., November 17, 1897.

CONTENTS.

CONTENTS

PRIZE-FIGHTING IN THE SCHOOLS.

IF a gladiatorial show, after the ancient Roman style, were proposed in a Christian nation at the present day, the public taste would be offended and the public conscience shocked. Were a Christian community invited to attend a walking-match, a pugilistic combat, or a bull-fight, the majority would turn indignantly away from such cruel and debasing pastimes. Yet, while we scorn the grosser forms of vice, we may be deceived by its more refined displays. Are we not constantly witnessing in the daily conduct of the schools, in England and in America, especially at the great exhibitions and commencements, the bloodless slaughter of thousands of unoffending spirits, in a manner scarcely more excusable than was the butchery of men and beasts to make a Roman holiday? Cruelties are inflicted not upon beasts, but upon the tender feelings of youths and little children. The principles and methods by which a few are taught in all the schools to rejoice in triumphing over their companions will, upon examination, be found to harmonize rather with the practise of heathen and ruffians than with the spirit of Christian civilization.

On the occasion of the installation of Dean Stanley, a few years since, as Chancellor of St. Andrews University, in England, that distinguished Churchman and popular divine quoted as embodying the spirit of his remarks at that important hour the time-honored motto of the university, which is, when translated, "To aim at highest honors and surpass my comrades all." This motto is here introduced because it so aptly expresses the predominant sentiment of all the schools. It implies, when analyzed, that honor is the chief object of, at least, all scholastic endeavor, and that the best method of obtaining it, as well as the proper criterion of deserving it, is the surpassing of others.

Are the young to be taught that honor is

the essential good, the ambrosia of the soul,
the strength and delight of its highest life?
Is it the divinely appointed solace of unsatis-
fied spirits? If honor signify simply the love
and esteem of our fellow men, then may it be
an object of innocent desire; but what means
the word "highest," with which it is here as-
sociated? Do not "highest honors" for one
imply lower and lowest for all others? Whenever higher things for some necessitate and
depend upon lower things for others, the
higher should be foregone. We may not
make a pleasure of others' woes. That the
essence of this motto is not misjudged to consist in a desire to exalt self in preference to
others is shown by its latter half, which declares the aim to be "to surpass my comrades all." But why should one desire to
surpass another? Is there essential good in
excelling another? Can a generous spirit rejoice in the mortification or defeat of its fellow? Is one the better for making another
appear worse than himself? If it be replied
that the object is not to distress another by

defeat, but to promote personal merit, which
may be estimated by comparison, the answer
is ready. First, that our fellow-men have
never been declared by any competent authority to be criterions of excellence in us.
The great apostle Paul thought those "measuring themselves by themselves, and compar-
.ing themselves among themselves, are not
wise." Secondly, the very pith of the sentiment seems to be in the joy which one is to
experience in excelling others. The spirit of
this motto is not to be distinguished from
that which exults in victory on the field of
battle, and most exults when most of treasure
is captured and most of life destroyed; and
being thus engendered and fostered in the
young, has done more to fill the world with
envious rivalries, cruel hates, and deadly
strifes than perhaps any other unrecognized
child of Satan. Can he who loves his neighbor as himself wilfully defeat him in a contest, and then rejoice more at his own success
than he grieves for his neighbor's defeat?
Yet, almost universally in the schools, the

surpassing of others is made the chief evidence of merit and the sole ground of reward. It begins with the "turning down" and "standing head" of the infant class, and closes with the gold medal or the first honor at the end of the scholastic career. If those thus taught and accustomed to derive happiness from the misfortunes or the faults of others ever learn the charity and the self-sacrificing devotion to the good of others which characterize a noble nature, they must do so in spite of these teachings of their youth.

In support of these views let us examine the most popular method of inciting to diligence and promoting scholarship in the schools. That method is, almost everywhere, a system of what may be termed exclusive prizes. A system of prizes is exclusive when the number of prizes is less than the number of competitors. In every such case some are mathematically doomed to failure. Only so many of the whole number can obtain a prize, and success depends solely upon excel-

ling others. The result is, not that one suc-
ceeds and others fail, which might be the
case were a prize in reach of all, but, one suc-
ceeds *because* others fail. To obtain the prize,
one need not be worthy or faithful, but simply superior to others. Superiority alone
takes the prize. But is superiority ever a
proper criterion of merit, or a just ground of
reward, save where it is attained by more
faithful endeavors?

Consider the case where three prizes are
offered to a hundred students. All may
strive, but ninety-seven must be disappointed,
How shall we balance the rejoicing of the few
against the disappointment of the many?
Yet this is the inevitable result of an unnec-
essary device which engenders and rewards a
selfish ambition. If the object be to promote
general diligence in study, this plan must
signally fail; since perhaps a majority would
deliberately relax their efforts, and but few
make any positive exertion to obtain a prize
where the chances are ninety-seven to three
against them, and where success, with at least

seven out of ten, would be a moral impossibility. The effect of this plan upon many is the reverse of that which is intended, leading them to study less, in order to avoid the mortification of apparent defeat in a contest thus unfairly thrust upon them.

If it be intended only to promote excellence and reward high merit in a few, then may the wisdom of the end, as well as the justice of the means, be seriously questioned. Is it wise or just to aim at the high development of a few through the neglect or detriment of the many? Are not higher attainments for all rather to be desired than the highest culture for a few? If learning, like money, shows a natural tendency to accumulate as the possession of the few, shall a system of education, professedly designed for all, be operated so as chiefly to benefit the more intellectual? Those who are aptest to make high attainments need least stimulant to exertion. The dull boy must strive, if he strive at all, against inevitable fate. Any plan which rewards only the highest excellence must forever fail to reach the

mediocre multitude who most need to be
aroused to exertion. If it be said that the ap-
proval of friends and the consciousness of
mental improvement are sufficient for the
many, while additional premiums are given to
the few who excel, it may be answered that
the supposition that the few who gain the
prizes are really any more worthy of reward
than others is often wholly without foundation.

Indeed, the system of prizes is perhaps more
at fault in its moral equities than in its practical results. Any system which rewards mere
excellence, without regard to the circumstances under which it is attained, must be lacking
in moral propriety. Naturally the prizes will
go to those of superior native intellect, or to
those having enjoyed other advantages which
imply no merit in the possessor. Ancestry
for generations back, conversations heard or
questions asked around the family fireside in
childhood, a good teacher in early life, a dozen
or a hundred incalculable influences, may combine to decide who shall take the prize on a

great commencement day. Yet none of these are personal merits of the student. As well reward the boy whose father is richest, or whose mother is prettiest, as to assign premiums to those only who know most. Nothing can be a just ground of reward or punishment except voluntary conduct. Now, if the relative intellectual capacities and attainments of the several contestants could be ascertained, and due allowance could be made for all natural inequalities and circumstantial advantages, at the outset; and if at the end it could be seen just how much advancement each had made, then some approach toward justice in the assignment of rewards might be attained. Otherwise, the crowning of the highest can not be more just when intellectual attainment is made the standard of judgment than if physical height was made the criterion of merit. He who begins with two talents and ends with four is more meritorious than he who begins with five and ends with eight; yet according to the system which judges solely by final results, the latter would carry off the palm. All must admit that, unless the competitors are equal at the outset, no just estimate of exertion or progress can be made by applying a common standard at the end of the contest. One of superior mind may with little exertion outstrip another of inferior powers, though he exert them to the utmost. Are the bestowments of heaven and the gifts of fortune to be made the grounds of disparaging comparisons and odious discriminations among those who should be taught to love as brethren?

Besides all this, the offering of prizes, which a number are led to desire, and often expect, but which only a few can obtain, leads not only to disappointment to many, but to a suspicion of unfairness or fraud on the part of the proposer of the prizes or of the judges of the contest. Who ever heard of a distribution of honors or prizes which gave satisfaction to the students or to their friends? Those who strive for the prizes can not be made to understand why honest toil should not be crowned with its merited and expected reward. Nor should they be satisfied; for none should ever be led to desire, much less to expect, that which they can not obtain. This whole plan of measuring students by their fellows is erroneous and harmful in high degree. It has fostered discontent, jealousy, envy, and even malicious hatred among the young, who have, to their sorrow, found these evil passions growing stronger in later years. While it has highly honored and sometimes overstimulated a few, it has mortified the spirits and weakened the energies of thousands who most needed quickening and encouragement. Often the body of the students seem chiefly used as foils to set off the shining qualities of a few whom nature or accident has made the smartest scholars in school. But to use the mediocre multitude only as stepping-stones to honor for a few brilliant intellects must ever be as unfortunate in result as it is unjust in principle.

This subject is of sufficient practical and ethical importance to justify some inquiry as to the opinions of the ancients concerning it.

Homer, the faithful mirror of the Grecian soul, represents Achilles as instituting various

2

contests during the festivities which were observed in honor of his departed friend Patro-
clus.   On these interesting occasions the number of prizes and the number of competitors
are invariably the same. The rewards are never
too few for every honest aspirant to receive
some token of appreciation from the distribu-
tor of prizes.   If five ambitiously contend in
the chariot-race, five separate rewards must be
theirs at the end.   If two engage in a boxing-
match, the victor of course claims the first
prize; yet sympathizing friends could not see
the vanquished depart without some consola-
tory proof of their appreciation of the manly
part he bore in the contest. They reckoned,
not without reason, that fate had decreed that
one or the other should be defeated, but felt
that failure in such a case was far from being
a proof of inferior merit.

So, too, in wrestling, in foot-racing, in fen-
cing, and in contests in archery; no more
competitors were said to enter the lists than the
number of premiums offered. The rule was varied from only in the single instance in which

a huge mass of iron became the property of him who could throw it farthest, which exception rather confirms than violates the rule; since the mass doubtless had many successive owners, and was valued only as a means of testing the strength of any who might be disposed to heave it.

That those high-souled Greeks, though heathen, were not destitute of the capacity, nor wanting in the disposition, practically to enforce the nicest moral distinctions is so beautifully illustrated in the case of two who disputed for the prize at the close of a chariot-race, that the passage deserves to be quoted. One, it appears, had, in a narrow pass, pressed his chariot-wheels against those of his competitor, and, by means which seemed not fair, had rushed into the way ahead of his rival. Was he, though victor in fact, entitled to the preferred prize? After some discussion, the one who thought himself wronged thus appealed to his opponent:

What Greek shall blame me, if I bid thee rise,
And vindicate, by oath, th' ill-gotten prize?

Rise, if thou dar'st, before thy chariot stand,
The driving scourge high lifted in thy hand;
And touch thy steeds, and swear, thy whole intent
Was but to conquer, not to circumvent:
Swear by that God whose liquid arms surround
The globe, and whose dread earthquakes heave the
  ground.

These direct and solemn words evoked a conscientious response; the wrong-doer confessed his wrong and freely yielded the prize he had unfairly won.

Though Virgil may have imitated Homer in many things pertaining to the style and structure of a heroic poem, yet we may not suppose him to misrepresent the moral sentiments of the age in which he lived. He describes Æneas as conducting certain games in honor of his father's memory on the anniversary of his departure to the land of spirits. On this grand occasion, the contestants in the ship-race, the foot-race, the boxing-match, and in shooting at the flying pigeon, "to the mast's high pinnacle confined," received, each one, whether many or few were engaged, a suitable reward. As he invites the eager multitude to enter the foot-race, hear him magnanimously exclaim: "Not one of you this day shall leave the field without his due reward!"* Such kind and considerate regard for the feelings of all who should honestly enter the race is in strange contrast with the cold and heartless literary contests of modern times. Those heathen could not bear to see a single one who had honestly striven go unrewarded away; but Christians, in this day, can witness with delight the mortifying disappointment of a hundred sensitive spirits, if one may exult in the selfish possession of a prize. We wonder that they should have enjoyed the gladiatorial shows, where men with beasts contended, but we delight to witness competitive examinations, prize declamations, and all that round of crucial conflict, in which the children and youth of our land are trained to appear, for the public delectation, at least once a year. What if feelings are publicly wounded, hopes disappointed, aspirations nipped in the bud, and sweet expectations drowned in the applause of

* Nemo ex hoc numero mihi non donatus abibit. ("Æneid," Book V., v. 305.)

the victor's merits? We have discovered the
best; we laud and reward them, and what care
we for the rest? The obedient herd are brought
before the multitude to be crowned or crushed,
and joy stands tiptoe when strong ambition
drags feebler merit in triumphal display before the public gaze. Is not the popular ma-
nia for intercollegiate contests in baseball and
football the legitimate outcome of such methods of teaching? A player's life, crushed or
kicked out in the reckless and ruthless strife
upon the field, is not a too costly, nor (shame
to tell!) a very uncommon, price to pay for
the empty privilege of huzzaing for the victo-
rious team. One vitiating principle of conduct inculcated in youth may be expected to
corrupt and poison all the motive forces of the
entire after-life.

It is readily admitted that it is much easier
to discover errors than to correct them, to
point out the faults in a system than to show
a more excellent way. I suggest that no rewards be offered to students but such as it is
both mathematically and morally possible for

all to obtain. The dull and the idle need most
to be quickened and energized, yet these are
apt to be affected not at all, or only injurious-
ly, by exclusive premiums. That a few brilliant and ambitious minds should exhibit on
special occasions the most admirable results
of diligence and high culture is a far less important achievement in the great cause of education than that hundreds of mediocre and
unaspiring souls should be raised to a higher, though not the highest, level, and be
made to feel that the world recognizes in them
mental and moral powers as appreciable and
as indispensable to the welfare of our race as
any possessed by those who are regarded as
most gifted of mortals. The plan of specially
honoring exclusively the best must forever re-
press the humble aspirations of the conscious-
ly inferior mind. It must, too, forever remain
chargeable with injustice, unless it can be
shown that the inferiority is in each case the
fault of its subject. Doubtless the Omniscient
Eye as much approves the faithful use of
humble powers as the achievements of the

mightiest minds. The gifts are God's, and those who use them, too, and he who uses best his gift is worthiest. A true mother bestows most care and appreciation on the least gifted of her children. Nor should those who are training souls for immortality base their plans upon any other principle. To ignore the truth that low attainments may be as worthy of reward as high ones is, in many instances, to injure the innocent and wrong those who are without defense.

This plan of measuring every man by others tends to engender a heartless and insatiable ambition, which only feeds upon victory, not over himself, but over one's neighbor. The youth who has spent his school-days in the atmosphere of such teaching enters manhood with the idea that he must surpass somebody or be nobody. Hence, among men of all trades, professions, and callings, jealousies, envies, and bitter animosities are but the legitimate fruit of early training. The ambitious soldier ruthlessly destroys the lives of others; the ambitious student unwittingly destroys his own.

Even into the sacred desk this unhallowed passion has crept, and the minister of the gospel, half unconscious of its sway, has overtasked his powers, not to save souls, but to gain reputation or surpass others; and by slow but surely suicidal steps offers himself an untimely sacrifice on the altar of ambition. Indeed, whenever and wherever an unholy ambition has destroyed the peace of individuals or families, broken the harmony of communities, or overthrown the liberties of nations, there may be seen the ripened fruits of this pitting policy of the schoolroom.

The negative results of ambition, though not so striking, are often as real, and possibly as abundant, as its positive effects. Though it drives one to do and dare, it suspends another's energies entirely. He will move neither hand nor foot nor tongue in any good cause if he see not a prospect of excelling another or of outdoing and triumphing over his neighbor. If he can not do some great thing, he will do nothing. The foot says: "Because I am not the hand, I am not of the body." Mortified pride schismatically abandons its place, because it is thought not to be sufficiently high. The ear pines in discontent, because it is not the eye. It was the man of one talent who, half in envy, half in spite, and all in proud contempt of the meagerness of his gift, hid his lord's money in the earth.

As the Scriptures furnish confessedly the only perfect standard of morals, let light be sought from them on this vital question. Does the Bible in any place teach that one man should strive to excel another; or make one man's conduct or attainments the standard by which others are to be judged? Can the idea of rewarding one for excelling another be found in the Book? Did the great Teacher ever utter a word to suggest or encourage strife for preeminence among his followers? Does any New Testament writer hint such a doctrine? The apostle Paul was driven into boasting by the influence of certain false teachers. Yet where else can such a piece of sarcasm be found as that in which he defends his folly, declaring that he "speaks not after

the Lord, but as it were foolishly;" not from
choice, but because they had compelled him.
For their sakes, though to his own disgust, he
parades his unparalleled sufferings and proclaims his "visions and revelations of the
Lord," avowing, nevertheless, that he was a
fool in thus glorying, and that, though in nothing was he behind the very chiefest apostles,
yet was he nothing. The spirit of Biblical
teaching is, everywhere, that we are not to
seek our own good in preference to another's.
We are to love our neighbor as ourselves, and
to "look not every man on his own things, but
also on the things of others." "In honor," we
are exhorted "to prefer one another." How
unanswerable is the Saviour's question, "How
can ye believe, which receive honor one of another, and seek not the honor that cometh
from God only?" All the life of Jesus Christ
on earth was a sacrifice of himself for the good
of others; but in order to make us realize the
power of this great truth as no mere words
could do, he proceeded to lay down his life for
us, and, says the apostle John, " we ought to

lay down our lives for the brethren." The contrast between the spirit of these teachings and that which makes a struggle for preeminence the life of the schools is strong and painful. Children may play and sit and eat together in peace, but the great object for which they are sent to school must be accomplished only through an endless conflict for place, honor, or reward. None is to be satisfied while another is head. Consequently only one can be satisfied in the largest class. What angry looks, what despairing countenances, what weeping faces have we seen in the schoolroom, under the ruthless operation of this baneful system! I wonder what the teachers thought when a little girl overtaxed her brain striving to commit to memory the greatest number of verses to recite in Sunday-school, and died, it was supposed, of fever produced thereby!

Away with such a system, with its selfish motives, its exclusive rewards, and its unjust standards of merit; and let a system of truth and equity, which appreciates and rewards the merits of all, take its place. As well punish only the worst, as reward only the best. Let duty be enthroned as the aim, the guide and the measure of effort; as the motive, the rule, and the criterion of merit in scholastic and in all other life. Duty is, as the word implies, that which we owe to God, our neighbor, and ourselves. While no standard of duty can be perfectly understood or applied in our present degenerate state, yet the word of God, interpreted and applied by the conscience of man, is at once the most comprehensive and the most simple to all who have that word; to all who have it not, a purblind conscience becomes the author of many errors. Conscience is not an originative but simply a discriminative faculty, exhibiting as in a spectrum the elements of duty involved in the facts held by the intellect. While conscience is by no means infallible, and can never be above or contrary to the knowledge of each individual, it is in all cases the only possible guide in morals. Let every student study because duty to self, to parents, to mankind, and to God requires it, not because some other student studies. Let progress be measured from each pupil's former status, and merit be determined by the steady efforts and advance of each, not by one's outstripping another. The system which drags one forward and holds another back, to suit the pace of a third, is injurious to all. Only so far as a man does his duty is he useful in the world. The young can not, then, be too early trained to act from a sense of duty. No principles should prevail in the schoolroom but such as should hold stronger sway in future life. If knowledge is power, too much care can not be taken that such moral principles shall accompany its acquisition as shall insure its rightful use. If ambition should be the mainspring of conduct, then let it be made strong in the young; but if it is the bane of manhood, it is the poison of youth.

There are two great systems of morals in the world: the theistic and the empirical. The former makes accountability to God the basis of conduct; the latter makes present expediency the criterion of right. Never was there a time when Christians had more need to guard with jealousy the spirit and conduct of all educational appliances. In several European nations, and in this country, the state provides education for the public. The state professes no religion, and can teach none. The result of the theory may be, as is evidenced by several foreign countries, a godless education and a nation of skeptics and infidels. Most of the teachers in our public schools are Christians now, but this may not always be the case. When Christian principles and good moral character shall be no more a necessary qualification for a teacher of a public school than they now are for a sheriff or a juror, what then will become of morals in the schools? President Grant proposed, in exact accordance with the spirit of our government, to exclude the Bible from public schools. It is not now taught, if read at all, in one out of ten public schools. Can such schools satisfy Christian people? The Churches should maintain and multiply, with increasing zeal and liberality, the large number of literary institutions under their control; and see to it that duty to God, our neighbor, and ourselves be made the fundamental rule of conduct in them all. If selfish ambition rule among the children of this world, let it not poison the fountains of Christian education. Let not sons and daughters go out from our schools filled with an insatiable ambition, but thoroughly taught and trained to obey the behests of duty. Ambition is never satisfied, and is ever disappointed; duty often realizes more than its moderate expectations. Ambition lays its plans, and claims God as the Author of them; duty seeks only to make God's plans her own. Ambition enslaves us to a dominant passion; duty subjects us to divine commands. Duty holds our powers under gentle and constant sway; ambition drives with impetuous and exhausting fury. Duty is a spirit from on high; ambition is a fury from the pit. Duty would serve, but ambition would rule. There is neither piece nor rest to the ambitious soul, but the dutiful spirit is kept in perfect peace.

"Duty is the sublimest word in the English

language," said Robert E. Lee, as he passed from the battle-field of failure in his country's cause to the peaceful toils of the schoolroom. He who would pronounce the man less worthy, or his achievements less meritorious, because he was not successful in conquering his opponents must surely be lacking in the best elements of judgment. To fail as he did was certainly nobler and better than to succeed as many have done. The theory which makes superiority alone the test of merit in the schools is quite of a kind with that which makes might the sole arbiter of right in the social and political spheres. Yet the latter principle is so abhorrent to the dictates of justice that none would avow it, and none but tyrants would act upon it. Away, then, with the system of strife and injustice, and let duty's wholesomely energizing power be diffused through all the schools. Instead of the selfish and vindictive spirit of the motto quoted in the outset, which proclaims a purpose to surpass all others and claim the best for itself, let the motto rather be, *to improve all my*

3

time and powers, and do my duty in all things.
Let *"Duty"* be the motto of the school, the inspiration of the student, and the talisman
against all foes and failures in coming life. Let
the honest youth inquire not " How I shall excel all others? " but " How shall I make the best
use of all my powers?" how shall I answer the
ends for which I was created? and how shall I
secure for my own conscience and from all who
know me, the wholesome and not uncharitable
plaudit, ' *Well done?* ' " Thus, by "mounting
on the shoulders of our former selves," and
not by riding over others, shall we advance in
learning and in all things for the best.

FILL YOUR OWN PLACE,

OR MORALS IN RHYME.

Nothing is ever done beautifully which is done in rivalship,
nor nobly which is done in pride.—*Ruskin.*

FILL your own place, and fill it well;
From royal throne to prison-cell,
'Tis worth, not birth, adorns each place
And helps to raise our fallen race.
Through discontent the angels fell
And found their proper place in hell.
The lives of toil and deaths of pain
Have brought mankind the greatest gain.
Who pineth for another's lot
The heavenly rule must have forgot,
That each shall his own burden bear,
And each shall feel his brother's care.
Who'd fill your place if you did not?
Perhaps you fill it to a dot.
Would you unto another give
The life designed for you to live?
Forego a glory all your own
In strife to seize another's crown?
There's need for what each soul can do,
The world is made complete by you.
The man whose state you most admire

May look on yours with strong desire.
The feet and hands, the ear and eye
In envy cry—in scorn reply—
They all are of one body parts,
Whiche'er is pained the other smarts.
Another turn in fortune's wheel
The proud man's fate for woe may seal;
Who once was rich, but now is poor,
Had better never known good store.
The tallest tree the storm strikes first,
And tears the richest foliage most;
The low, scant shrub bends and escapes
While desolation round it sweeps.
Then be thy lot or low or high
In sweet contentment live and die;
To do the work assigned to thee
Is as an angel's ministry.
Seek thou no place, no duty shun,
But be with Christ in Spirit one;
God will not praise you in that day
That you've crushed rivals by the way;
But if you've helped a helpless one,
Then you the noblest work have done.

FREEDOM, HUMAN AND DIVINE.

IF the will, which we find governs the members of the body, and determines their motions, does govern itself, and determines its own actions, it doubtless determines them in the same way, even by antecedent volitions. The will determines which way the hands and feet move, by an act of choice; and there is no other way of the will's determining, directing, or commanding anything at all. Whatsoever the will commands, it commands by an act of the will. So that the freedom of the will consists in this, that it has itself and its own actions under its command and direction, and its own volitions are determined *by itself.* It will follow that every free volition arises from another *antecedent volition,* directing and commanding that; and if that *directing* volition be also free, in that also the will is determined; that is to say, that directing volition is determined by another going before that; and so on, till we come to the first volition in the whole series; and if that first volition be free, and the will self-determined in it, then that is determined by another volition preceding that—which is a contradiction, because by the supposition it can have none before it. But if that first volition is not determined by

any preceding act of the will, then that act is not de-
mined by the will, and so is not free in the *Arminian*
notion of freedom, which consists in the will's self-
determination. And if that first act of the will be not
free, none of the following acts, which are determined
by it, can be free.

The above is taken from the famous work
of Jonathan Edwards on "The Freedom of
the Will and Moral Agency," first published
in 1853. By this work chiefly he acquired a
world-wide reputation as a metaphysician of
the highest order. Able transatlantic critics
pronounced him "the highest of all his con-
temporaries," and "perhaps unmatched, certainly unsurpassed, among men," in the field
of metaphysical argumentation. The above
is a select specimen of his strong and subtle
reasoning, according to which every act of the
human will is bound fast in the iron chain of
fate. But mankind need not consent to be
robbed of the "liberty wherewith God has
made us free," by even this masterly logic.
This argument presents a most remarkable
instance of what the logicians call begging
the question, assuming, as it does through-

out, the question in dispute. It is said: "If
the will determines its own actions, it *doubtless* determines them in the *same way* in which
it determines the motion of the hands and
feet—that is, by *antecedent volitions.*" No, not
doubtless, for there is grave doubt. Why is
the will properly said to govern the motions
of the body by antecedent volitions? Is it
not because the will itself must be supposed
to be external to and more or less distant
from each member of the body, and therefore
to require time and sequence for the trans-
mission of its orders to the different members
of the body? But this idea could not enter
into any proper conception of the self-deter-
mination of the will. Is not the will an indivisible unit? Would not its volitions, on the
supposition of its being self-governing, be
each spontaneous, instantaneous, untransmit-
ted, and independent of any antecedent, save
the existing mind? One of the chief difficul-
ties in connection with this question arises
from the lack of proper words, and especially
of proper illustrations by which to convey

our ideas. The Arminian holds the will to be free in a sense to which there is no analogy in the universe save in God himself. To set out, therefore, in the discussion of the freedom of the will, with conceptions and expressions of its action which imply constraint, is to beg the question at the start; and to illustrate the origination of its acts by those things which are confessedly under the control of others is not only equivalent to assuming what should be proved, but it is to fetter our own minds, while we befog and mislead the minds of all others who adopt the illustration.

It is even asserted that "there is *no other way* of the will's determining anything at all, except by antecedent volitions." Why not? That is the question. Says our author: "If that first volition is not determined by any preceding act of the will, then that act is not determined by the will; and so is not free in the Arminian notion of freedom." Here the *will* and an *act of the will* are confounded. If the will can not act without a preceding act of the will, then, if it acts at all, it must have been acting from eternity. Every act must have been preceded by another. There could have been no primal act. It is as much as to say, the will can not will without previously willing to will. All the acts of the will are first assumed to be related to each other, as the links in a chain, and then the possibility of a first link is denied, on the ground that there is no preceding link on which it may hang.

This argument rests upon the error of what Sir William Hamilton calls "a one-sided view of the finitude of the mind." By this method the infidel may easily prove, either that God as the great First Cause can not exist, or that he is himself the subject of eternal fate.

If we can not conceive how anything can exist without being dependent on something previously existing, then we can not conceive of God as a cause uncaused, and we should conclude, according to this mode of argument, that God does not exist. Likewise it may be argued that if the human will can put

forth no act that is not determined by a preceding act of itself, then every act of God is,
for the same reason, determined by a preceding act, and God is himself controlled by unalterable necessity, and that, too, a necessity
not arising from his moral attributes, but
natural, constitutional, and invincible. If
there is, then, any freedom in the universe—if
it be not a vast complex machine, moving
without a mover—there must be some other
way for wills to act than that to which Edwards would confine the Arminian notion of
freedom. If God is free, could he not make
man also free? Why may not the human
will be the source of volitions, as the sun is of
light? Does the sunlight of to-day depend
upon the sunlight of yesterday? Can not
God lodge power in man to be used, within
certain limits, as freely as God uses his own?
May not self-government be synonymous
with freedom? Our inability to conceive the
absolute commencement of volition is no argument against its possibility, since we are
equally unable to conceive the absolute non-

commencement or infinite regression of volitions. Volition in man must have had a beginning, or else man had no beginning. Why
not, then, admit that the will is free, in the
sense that its acts are not caused by anything
outside of itself, and that they are independent of all preceding acts or states of itself;
that it is a power which assimilates man to
his Maker, and renders him capable of accountability to God?

Very different conclusions from these of
Edwards may be reached by stating the argument thus: If the will governs itself, it
doubtless determines its own acts in a different way from that in which it controls the
members of the body, which are external to
itself. The actions of the body are determined by antecedent acts of the will, whose
influence is transmitted to its various parts
by those nerves which our Creator has sup-
plied for this purpose; but the will, being an
indivisible unit, can not be conceived as giving
orders to itself (except in a figurative sense
which requires the idea of plurality of parts

in the will), but must be supposed to act in a manner peculiar to itself. It is itself the fountain of action. It can act for or against any and all motives, and can not be forced by any power known on earth or revealed from heaven. Since, then, nothing can be thought to be the author of its own enslavement, and since our whole consciousness would be a lie and our accountability to God absurd, if our wills are controlled by any power outside of ourselves, we must conclude that the human will is sovereign in itself—the image of God in the soul of man. It is personality in man that wills and acts without compulsion. Otherwise his nature is a fraud and himself a machine or a slave.

If, however, according to the argument of some writers, God is himself the subject of necessity, then all support for the doctrine of human freedom, drawn from the supposed freedom of God, must fail. They maintain the freedom of man, as a probationer choosing and fixing a moral character; but deny freedom to God, as under subjective necessity to act just as he does. Yet it may be asked, if God's acts are determined, who or what determines them? God, or some other being or power? To say that the laws of his being determine them is not satisfactory. Are the laws of his being stronger than God? If so, how did they come to be so, and how do we know that they will continue to be so?

To say that God can not do otherwise than he does is to make him a machine. To affirm that he will not do wrong, and that his choice will ever be the manifestation and criterion of wisdom and goodness, is to ascribe to him his true glory. The Scriptures* declare that it is impossible for God to lie. No clear thinker

---

*Seneca, a Stoic, says: "Vir bonus non potest non facere quod facit; in omni actu par sibi, jam non concilio bonus, sed more eo perductus; ut non tantum recte facere possit, sed nisi recte facere non possit." Velleius Paterculus said of the younger Cato: "Homo virtuti simillimus, et per omnia ingenio Diis quam hominibus propior, qui nunquam recte fecit ut facere videretur, *sed quia aliter facere non poterat.*" (Farrar's "Early Days of Christianity," p. 629, note.)

would confound the impossibility here spoken of with that implied in the assertion, it is impossible for man to fly. The impossibility in the one case arises from physical inability; in the other, from moral indisposition. God will not lie, not because truth controls him, but because he maintains truth. It adds far more to God's glory to think that, having the power to do wrong, he will always do right, than to suppose that he does right because he can not do wrong. Can we not trust God with liberty?

There appears to be nothing gained by those metaphysical philosophers and theologians who seek to find a surer criterion of right and wrong, and a firmer basis for moral law, than the will of God. They have sought it in "the authority of the state;" in "something inherent in the nature of things," as "fitness," "truth," "relations," "moral beauty;" in "the highest happiness;" in "pride gratified by flattery;" in "an inner reciprocal sympathy;" in "the moral sense;" and in "intuition." Why thus tax their brains for something stronger, surer, clearer, or more authoritative than the will of God? If there is an essential fitness of things, did not God make that fitness? And does not God maintain that fitness? Did not God ordain our ideas of fitness? Could he not have made us to think otherwise of fitness than we do, had he so chosen? Who dare answer these questions in the negative? And are the things that are determined by the will of God more stable than that will itself? The objection to the will of God as the ultimate rule of right seems to be that it is arbitrary; and, therefore, conceivably changeable. Why should anything be thought more unchangeable than the free will of God? Any such supposition involves the idea that God is somehow under the dominion of an established order outside of himself, or at least that he is controlled by the immutability of his own attributes. Who can affirm that aught is immutable, but the will of God? And that immutability we hold, as we do God's existence, upon faith alone.

If, however, according to the teachings of

many moralists, the will of God is not the sole foundation of the moral law and the ultimate rule of right, it is certain no surer ground or rule can be found elsewhere. One says: "The law of God is supreme, unchangeable reason; it is unalterable rectitude; it is the everlasting fitness of all things that are or ever were created." How does reason become unchangeable, but by the will of God? Did reason establish itself without God, and above God? Who decides what rectitude is? How did we come to have our ideas of rectitude? Especially, what makes rectitude unalterable? Did it make itself so, or was it made so by our thoughts; or did God make it so? All such expressions as the above quotation seem almost meaningless, unless we suppose something to exist independent of God.

If all things, save God, were created, all laws of thought are the results of creative power; and, while we can not even imagine how we should have thought or felt about right or wrong, or aught else, had we been created differently, we surely can not limit God's power

or prerogative, and say that he could not have
made us to think fundamentally differently on
any or all subjects from what we now do.
Why, then, speak of "the everlasting fitness
of things?" How can "everlasting fitness"
be any better or stronger than the simple will
of God? Did things have a fitness before
they were made, or did not their fitness
arise from their relations as created? If, then,
God made the fitness of things, their fitness
only expresses his will.

*To undertake thus, even in thought, to guaran-
tee the moral stability of the universe by denying
freedom and absolute creative authorship, even of
moral distinctions, to God, is no gain to reason
and a great loss to faith.* Whenever we undertake to bolster the will of God by his attributes or by the postulates of reason, those
attributes or postulates will, in their turn,
require to be bolstered, and we gain nothing
in the end. As an origin of law, right, and
authority, there is nothing imaginable that
compares with the will of the Supreme Being.
All other sources of right and law seem to be

4

the mere figments of human fancy. We are compelled to come to the incomprehensible and absolute first cause somewhere. Why undertake to rob the Biblical theology of its preeminent excellence and simplicity, tracing, as it does, the origin and support of all things to the will of a personal God, by our vague and endless endeavors to find something more stable than the will of God? Every suggestion of anything superior to the will of God savors of pantheism, as when we say that a thing is right not because God wills it, but God wills it because it is right. Whence does the right come that rules God? Either from himself or some other being. If from another, then we have another and a superior God; if from himself, then it is but the expression of his will.

All these varied attempts to find other foundation for right and law than the will of God seem to be but the futile efforts of intellect to avoid the exercise of faith. Man would rather understand than believe. He prefers the pride of reason to the humility of faith. Yet he who will not believe where he can not understand can never take hold of the things of God. The exercise of faith is God's supreme requirement of man, and the utmost duty of the soul to its Maker. The sublime simplicity of faith is marred by the anxious, though futile, attempts of reason to supersede or support it.

Biblical philosophy stands contradistinguished from all other systems in ascribing to a personal God the origin, authorship, and absolute sovereignty in all things. The strongest and most laborious intellects of the ages have sought in vain for a more satisfactory foundation for that faith to which all must come at last, or wander "in endless mazes lost." Yet even some believers in the Bible have, as has been shown, allowed themselves to be led by the speculations of metaphysicians to seek for a better foundation for right than the will of God. In so doing they have abandoned their strength. The attempt of the ancients to account for the support of the world by the serpent on the back of the tortoise was not more futile than all attempts to find a basis for moral law outside the will of God.

Quite similar in origin and tendency is the doctrine which denies moral freedom to God. The Scriptures declare: "He doeth according to his will in the army of heaven, and among the inhabitants of the earth: and none can stay his hand, or say unto him, What doest thou;" "for he giveth not account of any of his matters." It has already been shown that nothing is gained by denying freedom to God. Let us now inquire what the divine oracles teach on the subject, not directly, but by necessary implication.

1. The fact that Adam was endowed at his creation with the capacity to choose moral good or evil is a demonstration of the moral freedom of his Maker. If, as is maintained, God is ever under subjective necessity to act in a certain way, and that the best possible, how is it conceivable that he could endow his creature, man, with the power of choosing and doing either good or evil? If any deny

that Adam was free to choose good, it is not proposed to reason with them now. That denial would lead to the doctrine of the eternity of matter, make the universe a machine, and God only a part of its matter or forces, sanction stoicism in philosophy, and lead to licentiousness for religion. But that Adam possessed the power to choose and do evil is incontestably proved by the fact that he exercised that power. Now it is inconceivable that God could produce in his creature, man, moral powers which he did not himself possess, and could not exercise if he chose. Could God impart to man a moral or other sort of power which he did not realize in his own being, or could not realize if he would? No powers can be supposed to reside in the creature which did not exist, actually or possibly, in the Creator. We may easily imagine the creature doing that which his Maker would not do, but not what his Maker could not do if he would. It is not forgotten nor overlooked that our opponents hold that the necessity which binds God to righteousness

is wholly subjective. The purpose to create
Adam was subjective, till it began to be realized objectively. That purpose embraced a
capacity of free choice in God's ideal of his
noblest earthly creature. Let him show who
can that God, if for any reason himself in-
capable of free moral choice, either could or
would endow his creature, man, with such
power. Yet Adam was so endowed, or else
fated to do wrong. If the latter be affirmed,
then must God be supposed not only to possess the power to do wrong, but to have ex-
hibited it through man from the beginning to
this day.

2. The Scriptures, in declaring that man was
made in the image of God, do virtually affirm
the moral freedom of God, in whatever sense
freedom may be admitted as belonging to
Adam. This argument must not be confounded with the preceding, for it is quite distinct.
Man might have been free and not in the image of God; or he might have borne the image
God and not have been free, if God were not
free. But, man being free, the first argument

inferred that his Maker was free; if, moreover, man was both free and in the image of God, this second argument *affirms* the unavoidable conclusion that his Maker must have been free also. All the force of the preceding argument passes into this, and herein receives the immense corroboration of the scriptural affirmation that man, free as he was, was the image of his Maker. Whatever we may suppose the image of God as existing in man to imply, we can scarcely imagine man's highest attribute, his capacity for moral freedom, to be excluded from that image. We can not but believe that the noblest attributes of man reflect most truly the image of his Maker. That image is usually supposed to consist in righteousness and true holiness. But to speak of a necessitated righteousness, or a compulsory holiness, is to speak irrationally, if not absurdly. If, then, the essential elements of the divine image in man do not exclude, but necessitate moral freedom, why should such freedom be thought to be an impossible or an unworthy attribute of God?

The conclusion then follows that, if man at his creation was morally free, his Maker must have been free also; or, if man was not free, he must have been somehow constrained by his Maker to the choice of evil, which assumption imputes a choice of evil rather than good to God; and he, being immutable, must forever continue to choose the evil and compel his creature, man, to practise it—a conclusion too monstrous and revolting to be affirmed. The only alternative is, that God is free as to the choice of moral good and evil, and that he so created man, who, by the abuse of his liberty,

"Brought death into the world and all our woe."

This supposition by no means jeopards the great doctrine of God's immutability, which must not be given up. How can we be more certain that God can not change than that he will not, though he can? His declared unchangeableness is simply a fact that challenges our faith. All attempts to guarantee it by seeking reasons in his attributes or in any conceivable relations of things seem utterly vain, setting out in a circle of secondary reasons, each of which requires another, till we are finally driven to the will of God as the ultimate and self-sufficient reason for all things. If it be asked why do two and two make four, or why am I obliged to tell the truth, the answer is, I am so constituted that I can not think otherwise in the one case, nor feel otherwise in the other. Could God have made me to think and feel otherwise? I dare not say that he could not. The relations of things result from their creation, and our apprehension of those relations and of the duties which those relations suggest arise from the adaptation of our minds to our surroundings. If we think in accordance with the true relations of things, we are sane; if we think otherwise, we are, to the degree of that erroneous thinking, insane. If we act in accordance with our true relations, we are good; if we act otherwise, we are bad. To ascertain the true relations of things to ourselves is but to learn the will of God concerning us. Conscience, or the moral sense, is that in man which renders him capable of realizing a feeling of obligation or duty in view of his relation to God and to his fellow beings. Hence every imaginable form of the rule of right amounts, in its application, only to a man's own judgment of what he ought to do. But the great underlying question is: " What ought a man to think to be right?" Is his conscience or his judgment of the fitness of things, or his sense of personal worthiness, always a safe guide? By no means. These are but the divinely appointed aids to man in his efforts to find out that which is undoubtedly the ultimate criterion of right, the will of God. This will may be learned from God's Word, or inferred from his works, or felt in the instinct of our souls, but is unquestionably the only ultimate rule both of our faith and our practise.

It is concluded, then, that God is not only free, but the author and perpetual maintainer of all truth, right, and law. He commands a thing not because it is right, or was right before he commanded it, but all his commands are the declarations of his will, which is the fountain, criterion, and law of right. Through the ages we expect God's commands to be consistent with all his previous works and words. This is, indeed, all that is really meant by the nature of things and the eternal fitness of things. Let it be remembered that things have no nature but what God gave them, and that things, as here spoken of, are not eternal, much less can their fitness be so, it being only the mutual adaptation of their relations and our ideas under the will of God. All mathematical as well as other truth rests upon the will of God for its basis. If there were no God, there would certainly be no outward universe. Whether numbers be regarded as objective realities, or subjective conceptions of the mind, without God there would neither be things to be counted nor minds to count them. If there were no God, two and two would not be four, for neither one nor two nor four would have any existence. But does our belief that two and two make four, as things are, depend upon the will of God? Undoubtedly it does. A crazy man might think otherwise. If any man denies that we owe the sanity of our minds to God's providential care, these reasonings are not for him.

Suppose that in answer to the question, "Shall not the judge of all the earth do right?" it should be replied, "In many things God does wrong." Would not such an answer be futile? "Who art thou, O man, that repliest against God?" Shall a man argue against the standard of right, or think against the criterion of thought? Indeed, some do presume to arraign God's word and works for condemnation.

If the above question be supposed to imply that liberty, then may God be put under condemnation by his creatures, and the sovereign of the universe stand guilty at the bar of human reason.

Is not the question rather a challenge for men to perceive and admire the righteousness of God? We can conceive of God as doing wrong only by acting out of harmony with himself. Our judgment of right and wrong springs from the constitution of our minds as affected by all that is about us. *We expect constancy and consistency in God; but if we should suppose that we had discovered aught to the contrary, our thoughts should be corrected by his will and works, and not his will and works by our thoughts.* " He is before all things, and by him all things consist." "Yea, let God be true, but every man a liar." If harmony, fitness, and truth bind God, he first established the harmony, designed the fitness, and gave to truth her being, her beauty, and her power; so that he is a law unto himself, which is the highest style of freedom. The will of God must forever remain the highest reason for itself, as well as for all things else, since whatever may be adduced to justify, sanction or support it must be reckoned among its creatures or dependencies.

THE RILL.

Lines found in the branches of a willow overhanging a pebble-bedded stream.

I go, I go, I gladly go,
Just where or why, I do not know;
For I have none the way to show,
And yet I must forever flow.
I hear a voice from far away—
I must be gone—I can not stay.
A saucy rill, I trip down-hill,
And in the shade lie cool and still;
I ripple o'er my pebbly way
Where minnows play the livelong day;
My birds make morn with music thrill;
At eve I wake the whippoorwill;
And when the stars send down their light
I kiss them every one good night.

I laugh and leap, I dash and sweep,
My joyous way I always keep;
I dance and run, I wait for none;
And, as gay rills have always done,
I snatch warm kisses from the sun
And dash them everywhere for fun.

I sometimes wind and sometimes creep,
And then I turn and sneak and seep;
And when you hear me murmuring low
Then something tries to make me slow.
Things do provoke and try me so
I hardly know which way to go.
I curl and purl and twist and twirl,
And then dart off in merry whirl;
I glide, I slide, and try to hide,
And though I'd shun the pomp of pride,
I rise and swell and leap and fall,
And still go onward after all.

The children free play oft with me;
I join in all their artless glee;
With glad'ning sights and merry sounds
My liquid life for aye abounds.
Oft, too, to me the aged come back
To tread again in childhood's track,
But eye and ear and joy's glad tone
With lapse of years are dimmed or gone.
Man cometh forth, grows old, and dies,
But my fresh fountain never dries;
All gladness flows and grows with me,
Forever new, forever free,
While man and beast and bird and bee
Take draughts or drops at will from me.
When summer suns with burning heat

Drive famished herds to my retreat,
The sweltering kine wade to their knees
And bathe and drink and breathe at ease.

Slip o'er the hill just when you will,
And though you find me lying still,
Yet come close by and take a peep,
And you'll not find your love asleep.
I've often seen you passing by,
And oft your going made me sigh;
Why don't you stop and dip your feet?
My touch would be to them so sweet.
I'd make you long, e'en in your dream,
To spend your days beside my stream.
If you'll come near and look at me,
You'll on my breast your picture see;
And your sweet face shall then be mine,
And I shall with your beauty shine,
The happiest stream in all the land
To have so fair and fond a friend;
And so we will our graces twine,
And you shall be my Valentine.

MRS. SUSANNA WESLEY.

THE original constructor of the engine is the real author of the power and motion of the train. The molder of a character is the maker of a destiny; and whoever imparts transcendent qualities to a human soul cooperates with the Divine Being in promoting the highest good of our race. The mother who brings into the world and trains a child who shall marshal the great forces of humanity on the side of truth and right, who shall quicken and enlarge the better thoughts of millions, or who shall inspire or fitly express those nobler sentiments by which mankind are raised toward the higher ends of life, deserves herself to be ranked among the great ones of the earth. To have been the mother of one such man as either John or Charles Wesley was enough to command for any woman more than a common regard; to have been the mother of them both entitles

5

Susanna Wesley to a double portion among the children of honor forever. Among these originating and determining forces which produced and guided the great religious movement of the last hundred and fifty years called Methodism, the mother of the Wesleys must not be uncounted. Occupying during her life only the ordinary sphere of her sex, she so filled her place as mother and mistress in her home as to transmit a more powerful and permanent influence for good than perhaps any other human being of her day. She planted the handful of corn upon the top of the mountain, the fruits whereof did shake like Lebanon. She trained a lawgiver whose self-enforcing, because conscience-quickening, rules for holy living were to regulate myriads —yea, millions of the noblest lives on two continents, and whose influence is destined, no doubt, to spread throughout the world. She tuned the harp whose divine strains were to gladden and bless all hearts, and go echoing down the centuries, waking slumbering souls to the dread of hell and to the hopes of

eternal life. As the gentle and genial sun-
beams silently permeate the atmosphere, and
muster the forces that move in the sweeping
tornado or murmur in the storm that shakes
the earth, her forming hand and her inform-
ing spirit wrought wondrous things in her
two sons, brewing the gospel thunder and the
poetic lightning which were to startle the
English Church and rouse the careless world
to a new sense of duty and of God.

It is not surprising to find evidence that so
extraordinary a woman owed much to he-
reditary endowments. To doubt the possible
moral improvement of our race and the cu-
mulative enhancement of all our nobler powers through the transmitted results of ancestral growth in intelligence and virtue is to
doubt the persistent prevalence and final triumph of good over evil in this world. Mrs.
Wesley was honorably descended, being a
daughter of the celebrated Dr. Annesley, who
was one of those clergymen who at the time
of the Revolution preferred ejectment from
their places to the subjection of their con-

sciences to the dictation of the government. He was indeed one of the most remarkable men of his times, especially for his zeal and popularity as a preacher and for his helpful kindness to the dissenting ministers of his day. His daughter Susanna had a superior mind, and was well educated not only in English but also in the Latin, Greek, and French. She was pronounced intelligent, amiable, beautiful, and pious. Her faculties were too evenly balanced to suggest any claim to genius, which usually consists in certain admirable extravagances of intellect, which are apt to be accompanied by corresponding deficiencies. She was much disposed to think for herself, and for a time became involved in metaphysical speculations which interrupted the constancy of her Christian faith. Though her father was, and continued to be for fifty years, a most devoted, self-sacrificing, and useful minister among the Dissenters, she of deliberate choice became a member of the Established Church. Her doctrinal speculations and aberrations—for she wandered for a

time amid the errors of Socinianism—together with her change of Church relations, show,
to say the least, her independence of character.
At about twenty years of age she was married
to Rev. Samuel Wesley, a minister of the Established Church, and afterward for many
years rector of Epworth. He was a man
who, though not devoid of many great excellences of character, was yet better fitted by
many of his habits and mental peculiarities
for celibacy or for heaven, than for the care
of a large family of children on this mundane
sphere. He spent the chief part of his time
in "beating rimes," as he expressed it, in
writing and preaching sermons, in dispensing
charity beyond his means, and in rousing
wrath by the indiscreet assertion of his High-
church and royal preferences, never taking
due care that bread should increase with the
increase of his family. His picture shows a
man who looked to heaven, to the exclusion of
earth. His wife was compelled to manage
the temporal interests of the family—he had
no turn for practical affairs. The years of

Susanna Wesley's married life became years
of increasingly burdensome toil. The story
of her domestic struggles reads like the tale of
a beleagued garrison. She was the mother of
nineteen children, thirteen of whom were living at the same time. Notwithstanding the
poverty and even want in which they often
lived—enough to have crushed the spirit of
any but one of the truest heroines the world
ever produced— the order and discipline of
her household were a model for all who came
after her. A historian tells us: "The income
of the rector of Epworth was comparatively
small, and his children were very numerous.
Twice the parsonage house was unfortunately
burned down, and rebuilt at his own expense.
His circumstances, therefore, were painfully
embarrassed, and the children were far from
having any superfluity of either diet or cloth-
ing." In a letter dated January 20, 1722,
Mrs. Wesley says to her brother, Mr. Samuel
Annesley: "Mr. Wesley rebuilt his house in
less than one year; but nearly thirteen years
are elapsed since it was burned, yet it is not

half furnished, nor are his wife and children half clothed to this day." In answer to questions on the subject, she informed the Archbishop of York that she often experienced so much difficulty in obtaining bread, and in paying for it when it was obtained, as nearly equaled the pain of destitution. Indeed, it may be inferred from all our information on the subject that the Wesley family at Epworth often knew not one day how or where their living for the next was to be obtained. Constantly harassed and once imprisoned for debt as the father was, he yet failed, during his frequent absences from home attending the convocation in London, and on other public duties, duly to appreciate the pinching poverty and unshared toils of the mother who was giving her life to and for the children at home. Seldom, if ever, has the Biblical doctrine that "it is good for a man that he bear the yoke in his youth" found a more signal illustration of its beneficent results than in the Wesley family at Epworth; for surely never did a mother know better than Susanna

Wesley how to develop strength by the judicious application of the burdens of poverty and the restraints of law, or how to sharpen wits at the grindstone of want. Amid the distress of her situation, God was her constant trust and helper. Her strength was from on high. "God," says she, "supports, and by his omnipotent goodness often totally suspends all sense of worldly things."

The family government at Epworth embraced, among other things, a school kept for many years in a room of the house set apart for that purpose. No hired teacher officiated in that school. It was in conducting this home school that Mrs. Wesley gave evidence of such superior good sense and skill as must forever entitle her to the admiration and the honor of mankind. At five years of age each child was taken into the schoolroom, and, with rare exceptions, was taught its letters in one day. It was then put immediately to spelling out words and to reading the Bible. The interminable analytical nonsense of b-a ba, b-i bi, b-o bo, and b-u bu, had no place in

her system of teaching. In setting her children to reading as soon as they learned the
alphabet she anticipated by a hundred and
fifty years the results of modern progress in
the art of teaching. The hours of school
were from nine till twelve in the morning and
from two to five in the afternoon. No girl
was put to sewing till she could read distinctly and correctly. The children were all so
trained in the nursery from birth that they
needed very little governing in school. The
exercises were opened and closed with singing, else how had proper early development
ever been given to Charles's unparalleled apti-
tude for metrical composition? Here was
trained the greatest hymn-writer the world
ever produced. "Every child's will must be
subdued while it is very young," says this
wise, because practically successful, expound-
er and illustrator of child-training; "for this
is the only strong and rational foundation of
a religious education, without which both
precept and example will be ineffectual."
Her children were taught to be quiet at fami-

ly prayers, and to ask a blessing by signs before they could kneel or speak. Each child was taken in turn to a place of private prayer, and was both taught to pray and commended to God. A sense of individual responsibility to God is the source of all personal piety. Here was inaugurated and maintained that sacred order of thought and action which qualified John to be what he afterward became: a reformer of the doctrines and lives of almost all Christendom. The world had an abundance of sound doctrine and much of wise and wholesome precept before the days of Wesley; but it had nothing so short, so simple, and so good a guide for holy living as the "General Rules" which John Wesley prepared for his United Societies. But whence came his ability to set forth such a formula for holiness? Were not the "General Rules," in spirit at least, like the words of King Lemuel, the prophecy which his mother had taught him? The family government at Epworth was the embodiment of Mrs. Wesley's idea of the teaching of God's Word. It was

the form of her effort to fashion her children
unto godliness. Let it not be thought that in
all this she was without sadder trials than
any that mere labor and poverty may bring.
Her spirit had triumphed over want when she
wrote to the Archbishop of York: "I have
learned that it is much easier to be contented
without riches than with them." The rectory
was a home church and family school as happy, notwithstanding many privations, as perhaps any home in England; but Mrs. Wesley
was not without the peculiar and deeper sorrows incident to parenthood. Then, as now,
not every worthy young woman could find a
worthy man for a husband. Some of her
daughters were very unhappily married, and
brought inexpressible grief to the mother's
heart. In the agony of her soul she congrat-
ulates those who lose their children in in-
fancy, declaring that "it is better to mourn
ten children dead than one living, and I have
buried many." Ten of her nineteen children
reached adult years, and all became devoutly
pious and died in the Lord.

But Mrs. Wesley had another and scarcely a less important sphere of influence than that of the domestic circle. If Methodism found its cradle at Epworth, there also it was taught to walk. While her husband was away discharging the onerous duties of his calling, Susanna began to gather the poor neighbors with the children on Sundays, and to "read sermons, pray, and converse directly with the people" on religious topics alone. Learning this through her letters, her husband remonstrated with her for so unauthorized a procedure. When he asked why not let some one else read, she replied: "You do not consider what a people these are. I do not think one man among them could read a sermon without spelling a good part of it, and how would that edify the rest? Nor has any of our family a voice strong enough to be heard by such a number of people." Her audience grew to two hundred or more. Some complained against the assembly as a conventicle, but she pleaded for the privilege of teaching the common people, who, as when the Saviour spoke it, "heard the word gladly." Her services were calling out people not accustomed to attend public worship. They were filling up the parish church, gathering in the straying, and bringing many sinners to hear the gospel and seek the Lord. When her husband insisted that she should discontinue these meetings, she begged him to relieve her of the responsibility of that act by assuming it himself. "Do not advise," she said, "but command me to desist." Here was the spirit which, carried to its legitimate results, as it was in her sons, gave Methodism to the world. Here was conscientious conviction of duty yielding only under compulsion to opposing authority. Such a spirit, not wisely regulated, might lead to fanaticism and violence; but under proper guidance, it moves, reforms, corrects, and sanctifies the world. It is the same spirit as that which moved Peter and John to cast upon the council at Jerusalem the fearful demand, "Whether it be right in the sight of God to harken unto you more than unto God, judge ye." When in after-years John Wesley, her son, returning from one of his preaching tours, hurried home under mingled grief and displeasure at hearing of the irregular conduct of Thomas Maxfield, who had violated the order of the Church by preaching without authority, she said to him: "John, take heed what you do to that man, for he is as much called of God to preach as you are." Thus does she become—not only by her example before her children at Epworth, but by her counsel to John at the critical moment— the author of that system of lay preaching without which Methodism could never have been.

Comparatively few of the ministers of the Established Church ever became Methodists. The great body of its heroic preachers were laymen. The Church would not grant them orders. Wesley, with the views which he held during all the early period of Methodism, could not ordain them. They must preach as laymen or not at all. The mother's advice prevailed—he let them preach, and the instrumental power that was to fill the world with the theology, the hymns, and the worshiping assemblies of Methodism took its origin and form under the example and advice of Susanna Wesley; for, be it remembered, John Wesley obeyed his mother to her dying day. His intellect never outgrew hers far enough to suggest any better way. But let us understand she simply embraced life's opportunities as they were presented. She filled her place; she obeyed God. The world was ready for Methodism. The ungodly clergy and the backslidden and worldly membership of the Church needed it. Mrs. Wesley did not hinder, but helped, its coming. As her sons John and Charles traversed England preaching to assembled thousands on commons, in the streets, and in every place, the everlasting gospel, while the kingdom almost literally resounded with the roar of persecuting mobs and the shoutings of multitudes as they heard for the first time the glad tidings of salvation, I imagine the mother " kept all these things in her heart, and pondered them," even as Mary of old did the things spoken concerning her son. She had trained her sons for their work.

Luther's Reformation pertained chiefly to ecclesiastical authority and doctrine; Wesley looked rather to the spiritual interpretation of the Word, and to practical holiness of life. Luther reformed the body of the Church; Wesley, the soul. While John Wesley was at Oxford he became favorably impressed with the Arminian system of theology, as contra-distinguished from the prevalent Calvinism of that day. His mother, as he informs us, greatly encouraged and confirmed him in the adoption of that system, which through him afterward became the doctrinal foundation of Methodism. We are left to imagine the extent of her influence over him in this matter, but may believe it to have been great, as she abhorred Calvinism. Her system of teaching was both progressive and fruitful. It can scarcely be doubted that the admirable form of godliness in which she trained her children led to that extrordinary power which afterward attended the preaching of her sons. Hear her, as her spirit, soaring above all earth-born woes, utters sweet notes of triumph and repose: "Oft my mind emerges from the corrupt animality to which she is united, and by a flight peculiar to her nature soars beyond the bounds of time and place in contemplation of the invisible Supreme, whom she perceives to be her only happiness, her proper center, in whom she finds repose inexplicable, such as the world can neither give nor take away." A mother who amid the cares, burdens, and perplexities of a numerous family could employ such a style and utter such sentiments as these must have been possessed of a very superior mind as well as of a transcendent faith. There is a sound of the sermons of John, and of the hymns of Charles, and of the watchword of Methodism through the centuries in that sentence. But the fruit of the seed was richer and sweeter than that from which it grew. She gave to her sons the alabaster box of the gospel, thinking its costly contents too precious for common souls, till they broke it and filled her own heart, as well as the hearts of thousands more, with the unspeakable joys of the witness of the Spirit.

6

Let us now briefly recall a few of the more marked features of Methodism in its incipiency, and inquire as to Mrs. Wesley's connection therewith.

1. Methodism was an offshoot of the Church of England. It may be doubted whether it was morally possible for Methodism to have originated outside of the Established Church. Had it been possible for a Dissenter to have conceived its peculiar doctrines and polity, it would have been quite impossible to give them form and life outside of the national Church. The state Church was the grand trunk from which this vigorous branch derived the essential elements of its early life. Had Methodism begun in dissent, it would no doubt have been crushed in the bud. If these views be correct, how remarkable is the fact that both Susanna Annesley and Samuel Wesley, long before their marriage, and without any consultation with each other, should each have renounced dissent and joined the Established Church most unexpectedly and unaccountably even to their most intimate friends!

Was it the design of Providence that John and Charles Wesley should be born in the national Church? Could such irregular outdoor preaching as they and their unordained coadjutors conducted throughout the kingdom for fifty years have been tolerated elsewhere than under the shadow of the Establishment?

2. Itinerancy and lay preaching were of the formal essence of Methodism. The paternal grandfather of John and Charles Wesley was through life an itinerant preacher who refused orders to the end of his useful career. If the two grandsons inherited from him the peculiar aptness to heed the Saviour's command, "Go ye into all the world, and preach the gospel to every creature," yet the idea of lay preaching, which alone gave any real and permanent effect to that command, so far as Methodism was concerned, originated, both as a fact and as a doctrine, with their mother. Susanna Wesley was the first lay preacher of Methodism. Had she not conversed with her neighbors publicly on the subject of religion, and afterward defended Maxfield for do-

ing the same, lay preaching might never have been.

3. Methodism was an innovation which required for its establishment, besides many other great qualities of soul, inexhaustible patience, together with an invincible firmness and independence of spirit in its leaders. These Susanna Wesley, as well as her husband, possessed in a preeminent degree. As evidence of this fact, witness her early change of her Church relations, her demand for a " command to desist " from holding religious meetings with her neighbors, and especially her refusal to say "Amen " when her husband prayed in the family for a reigning prince whom she conscientiously believed not to be entitled to the throne; whereupon her husband declared that if they could not have the same king they should not abide in the same house, and left his home for a twelvemonth, after which he returned in peace neither chiding the other with any fault in the matter. Such was the conscientious invincibleness of the parents of John Wesley; and was there

ever in any other man so full a combination
and so admirable a balance of high qualities
as in John Wesley? It is not strange that
critics find it difficult to discover the secret of
his power.

> Conspicuously great in every noble gift;
> Wonderful in all, preeminent in none.

A man who at eighty years of age could say
he had never felt low spirits an hour in his
life; who had traveled more, preached more,
and written more than any other man of his
day; who had with persistent courage pro-
voked and met the powers of the Church, the
fury of mobs, and the rage of hell in carrying
out the convictions of his conscience—must
have had no common blood in his veins.

4. But it is not so much in any special features of Methodism that we would expect to
find the impress of her whom Isaac Taylor
aptly styled its mother, as in that indefinable
and immeasurable influence by which she made
her sons capable of originating such a movement. Without such a mother such sons could
never have been. There can be little doubt that

the preeminent spirituality which character-
ized all the work of the sons was largely due to
those early impressions which they, perhaps
unconsciously, received from the spirit of that
mother who, "often found in the invisible Supreme her only happiness, her proper center,
and repose inexplicable, such as the world can
neither give nor take away."

In estimating the character of Mrs. Wesley
due emphasis should ever be laid upon that
which most distinguished her as a woman- I
mean her genius for family government. If
she was not a genius in the common acceptation
of the word, she surely possessed genius such
as has seldom been equaled, perhaps never
excelled, for the highest work of woman on
earth—that is, family government.

If lawmaking is the highest function of being, he who makes the wisest laws is the noblest being. That, too, is the wisest law which
may be made to affect the greatest number for
the greatest good. Judged by this standard,
Mrs. Wesley's code for family government
will bear comparison with the best that have

been framed by men. Applying as it does
the highest principles of government to the
regulation of human life in its earliest stages,
it anticipates all other laws in time, and if
properly enforced would supersede the necessity for nine-tenths of the laws of all nations.
Other lawmakers propose to restrain or guide
the evil passions and principles of men; she
proposes to purify the waters at the fountain
—suppress the beginnings of wrong, and train
the child instead of imprisoning or hanging
the man. The substitution of lawmakers,
teachers, governors, and executioners for parents, in the regulation of human society, has
been the bane of its welfare in all ages. A
child is the property, the trainable life of its
parents, whom God holds responsible for its
character. Parents are as much bound to
form the characters of their children aright as
they are to save them from malformation, star-
vation, or death from any cause. Parents are
the original sovereigns of the human race, and
the real arbiters of its destiny. Let it be borne
in mind that these rules are not so much an

imagined direction as to how chidren should be governed as an after-description of how Mrs. Wesley's large family were governed. Their excellence was proved by successful application. Let it be further noted that these rules are not more to be valued for the specific directions they contain than for the evidence they afford of an order of family government so systematic as to be capable of being distinctly set down in writing. Some systematic family government must be administered, or the children will be ruined. Were God's primal law for training children obeyed, the world would be speedily transformed; the nations would know themselves no more. Does not God require all human beings to pass through childhood for the specific purpose of having them trained? Shall the children of our race lose the divinest opportunities of their being through the neglect of their parents? Let all parents adopt Mrs. Wesley's rules or make better ones. Let a copy of them be framed and hung in every home. If not specially applicable in every family, they are so full of good suggestions that they can not fail to be helpful to every faithful parent. Let Susanna Wesley's code for the nursery be a talisman in every home.

Through John and Charles Wesley this code has modified the world as no other of its kind has done. The mind that planned and executed that code in her own home saw a kingdom shaken by its power before her death, and may now perchance look down from a higher sphere to see the face of Christendom changing under the influence of the heavenly doctrines which she taught her sons, and realize, what she could not while on earth, that those who believe in Jesus shall do greater works in his name than even Jesus ever did while he was on the earth. Well may Dr. Adam Clarke declare of the Wesley family: "Such a family I have never read of, heard of, or known; nor since the days of Abraham and Sarah and Joseph and Mary of Nazareth has there ever been a family to which the human race has been more indebted."

When Mrs. Wesley was dying she said to

her children, six of whom were with her: "Children, as soon as I am released, sing a psalm of praise to God." They did so, and the echoes of that song are still multiplying among the grateful millions whom Methodism has blessed with the gospel throughout the world.

Mrs. Wesley's rules for training her children are hereunto appended. They are creditable alike to her head and her heart. The "Mother of Methodism" could have left no more appropriate legacy to the Church than a statement of the "*method*" by which she trained its founders. By duly appreciating these rules we shall greatly benefit ourselves, ascribe worthy honor to her name, and preserve the fittest monument to her memory. They are thus stated by herself:

"The children were always put into a regular method of living in such things as they were capable of, from their birth, as in dressing, undressing, changing their linen, etc.

"When turned of a year old- and some before- they were taught to fear the rod and to cry softly; by which means they escaped abundance of correction they might otherwise have had, and that most odious noise of the crying of children was rarely heard in the house, but the family usually lived in as much quietness as if there had not been a child among them.

"As soon as they were grown pretty strong they were confined to three meals a day. At dinner their little tables and chairs were set by ours, where they could be overlooked; and they were suffered to eat and drink as much as they would, but not to call for anything. If they wanted aught, they used to whisper to the maid that attended them, who came and spake to me; and as soon as they could handle a knife and fork they were set to our table. They were never suffered to choose their meat, but always made to eat such things as were provided for the family.

"Mornings they had always spoon-meat, sometimes at night; but whatever they had, they were never permitted to eat at those meals of more than one thing, and of that sparingly enough. Drinking or eating between meals was never allowed unless in case of sickness, which seldom happened. Nor were they suffered to go into the kitchen to ask anything of the servants when they were at meat. If it was known they did, they were certainly punished and the servants severely reprimanded.

"At six, as soon as family prayers were over, they had their supper; at seven the maid washed them, and, beginning at the youngest, she undressed and got them all to bed by eight, at which time she left them in their several rooms awake; for there was no such thing allowed of in our house as sitting by a child till it fell asleep.

"They were so constantly used to eat and drink what was given them, that when any of them was ill there was no difficulty in making them take the most unpleasant medicine, for they durst not refuse it, though some of them would presently throw it up. This I mention to show that a person may be taught to take anything, though it be never so much against his stomach.

"In order to form the minds of children, the first thing to be done is to conquer their

will, and bring them to an obedient temper.
To inform the understanding is a work of time,
and must with children proceed by slow de-
grees, as they are able to bear it; but the sub-
jecting the will is a thing which must be done
at once, and the sooner the better; for by neg-
lecting timely correction they will contract a
stubbornness and obstinacy which is hardly
ever after conquered, and never without using
such severity as would be as painful to me as
to the child. In the esteem of the world they
pass for kind and indulgent whom I call cruel
parents—who permit their children to get
habits which they know must be afterward
broken. Nay, some are so stupidly fond as
in sport to teach their children to do things
which in a while after they have severely beat-
en them for doing. Whenever a child is corrected it must be conquered, and this will be
no hard matter to do if it be not grown head-
strong by too much indulgence. And when
the will of a child is totally subdued, and it is
taught to revere and stand in awe of the parents, then a great many childish follies and

inadvertences may be passed by. Some should be overlooked and taken no notice of, and others mildly reproved; but no wilful transgression ought ever to be forgiven children without chastisement less or more, as the nature and circumstances of the offense require.

"I insist on conquering the will of children betimes, because this is the only strong and rational foundation of a religious education, without which precept and example will be ineffectual; but when this is thoroughly done, then a child is capable of being governed by the reason and piety of its parents till its own understanding comes and the principles of religion have taken root in the mind.

"I can not yet dismiss this subject. As self-will is the root of all sin and misery, so whatever cherishes this in children insures their after wretchedness and irreligion. Whatever checks and modifies it promotes their future happiness and piety. This is still more evident if we further consider that religion is nothing else than doing the will of God and not our own; that the one grand impediment to our temporal and eternal happiness being this self-will, no indulgence of it can be trivial, no denial unprofitable. Heaven or hell depends on this alone; so that the parent who studies to subdue it in his child works together with God in renewing and saving a soul. The parent who indulges it does the devil's work makes religion impracticable, salvation unattainable—and does all that in him lies to damn his child, soul and body, forever.

"The children of this family were taught, as soon as they could speak, the Lord's Prayer —which they were made to say at rising and bedtime constantly—to which as they grew bigger were added a short prayer for their parents and some collects, a short catechism and some portion of Scripture, as their memories could bear.

"They were very early made to distinguish the Sabbath from other days before they could well speak or go. They were as soon taught to be still at family prayers and to ask a blessing immediately after, which they used to do by signs before they could kneel or speak.

"They were quickly made to understand that they might have nothing they cried for, and instructed to speak handsomely for what they wanted. They were not suffered to ask even the lowest servant for aught without saying, 'Pray, give me such a thing,' and the servant was chid if she ever let them omit that word. Taking God's name in vain, cursing and swearing, profaneness, obscenity, rude, ill-bred names, were never heard among them. Nor were they ever permitted to call each other by their proper names without the addition of brother or sister.

"None of them were taught to read till five years old, except Kezzy in whose case I was overruled and she was more years learning than any of the rest had been months. The way of teaching was this: The day before a child began to learn the house was set in order, every one's work was appointed them, and a charge given that none should come into the room from nine till twelve or from two till five—which were our school-hours. One day was allowed the child wherein to learn its let-

ters; and each of them did in that time know
all its letters, great and small, except Molly
and Nancy, who were a day and a half before
they knew them perfectly, for which I then
thought them very dull; but since I have observed how long many children are learning
the hornbook, I have changed my opinion.
But the reason why I thought them so then
was because the rest learned so readily, and
Samuel, who was the first child I ever taught,
learned the alphabet in a few hours. He was
five years old on the 10th of February; the
next day he began to learn, and as soon as he
knew the letters began the first chapter of
Genesis. He was taught to spell the first
verse, then to read it over and over till he
could read it offhand without any hesitation
—so on the second, etc., till he took ten verses
for a lesson, which he quickly did. Easter fell
low [came late] that year, and by Whitsun-
tide he could read a chapter very well; for he
read continually, and had such a prodigious
memory that I can not remember ever to have
told him the same word twice. What was yet
7

stranger, any word he had learned in his lesson he knew wherever he saw it, either in the Bible or any other book, by which means he soon learned to read an English author well.

" The same method was observed with them all. As soon as they knew the letters they were put first to spell and read one line, then a verse —never leaving till perfect in their lesson, were it shorter or longer. So one or another continued reading at school-time without any intermission, and before we left the school each child read what he had learned that morning, and ere we parted in the afternoon what he had learned that day.

"There was no such thing as loud talking or playing allowed of, but every one was kept close to their business for the six hours of school; and it is almost incredible what a child may be taught in a quarter of a year by a vigorous application, if it have but a tolerable capacity and good health. Every one of these —Kezzy excepted—could read better in that time than most of women can do as long as they live.

" Rising out of their places or going out of the room was not permitted, unless for good cause; and running into the yard, garden, or street without leave was always esteemed a capital offense.

" For some years we went on very well. Never were children in better order. Never were children better disposed to piety or in more subjection to their parents, till that fatal dispersion of them after the fire into several families. In those days they were left at full liberty to converse with servants—which before they had always been restrained from — and to run abroad and play with any children, good or bad. They soon learned to neglect a strict observation of the Sabbath, and got knowledge of several songs and bad things which before they had no notion of. That civil behavior which made them admired when at home by all who saw them was in a great measure lost, and a clownish accent and many rude ways were learned, which were not reformed without some difficulty.

" When the house was rebuilt and the children all brought home, we entered upon a strict reform; and then was begun the custom of singing psalms at beginning and leaving school, morning and evening. Then also that of a general retirement at five o'clock was entered upon, when the oldest took the youngest that could speak, and the second the next, to whom they read the Psalms for the day and a chapter in the New Testament as in the morning they were directed to read the Psalms and a chapter in the Old, after which they went to their private prayers before they got their breakfast or came in to the family.

"There were several by-laws observed among us:

"1. It had been observed that cowardice and fear of punishment often lead children into lying, till they get a custom of it which they can not leave. To prevent this, a law was made that whoever was charged with a fault, if they would ingenuously confess it, and promise to amend, should not be beaten. This rule prevented a great deal of lying.

"2. That no sinful action—as lying, pilfering, playing at church or on the Lord's day, disobedience, quarreling, etc.—should ever pass unpunished.

"3. That no child should ever be chid or beat twice for the same fault; and if they amended, they should never be upbraided with it afterward.

"4. That every signal act of obedience, especially when it crossed upon their own inclinations, should be always commended, and frequently rewarded according to the merits of the case.

"5. That if ever any child performed an act of obedience or did anything with an intention to please, though the performance was not well, yet the obedience and intention should be kindly accepted, and the child with sweetness directed how to do better for the future.

"6. That propriety [ownership] be inviolably preserved, and none suffered to invade the property of another in the smallest matter, though it were but the value of a farthing or a pin, which they might take from the owner without—much less against—his consent.

" 7. That promises be strictly observed, and a gift once bestowed—and so the right passed away from the donor—be not resumed, but left to the disposal of him to whom it was given, unless it were conditional, and the condition of the obligation be not performed."

I WONDER WHAT WERE CHILDREN MADE FOR.

I WONDER what were children made for!
Why, to be loved and trained and prayed for,
   And do their parents' will;
And whatever may be said of them,
The best old folks were made of them,
   And so God makes them still.

When once of old high place was sought for,
What was a little child then brought for,
   And seated mid the group?
Thus Christ would humble high ambition,
And honor those of low condition,
   And lift the childlike up.

If still you are a little child then,
Seek to be meek and true and mild then,
   And ready to obey;
For only such where'er you find them,
Do always well the part assigned them,
   And that's enough to say.

CHILDREN INVITED.

Come children, to the gospel feast,
    For such as you 'tis given;
Come, even though you be the least,
    And eat the bread of heaven.

"Suffer the little ones to come,"
    The world's Redeemer said;
He calls you to a heavenly home;
    Come, then, be not afraid.

He takes the babes into his arms,
    He blesses infant souls,
He keeps them from a thousand harms,
    Their lives his love enfolds.

You can not be too young to love
    A Saviour such as he,
And when you reach the home above
    With him you'll ever be.

APPEAL TO CHILDREN.

O CHILDREN, have you thought,
  That you may Christians be,
And please the gracious One who bought
  Your pardon on the tree?

That you may keep God's law,
  And do his holy will,
And from his Book instruction draw
  To keep you faithful still?

The children who obey
  Their parents in the Lord,
They please their Maker every day
  And keep his holy word.

Not reverend sire, nor sage,
  Nor rich, nor great, nor wise,
Nor faithful ones of any age
  Are dearer in God's eyes.

Repent then, while you may:
  Avoid correction's rod;
In early morn of childhood's day
  Give heart and life to God.

THE STUDY OF THE NEW TESTAMENT IN GREEK.

No greater honor was ever conferred upon a human language than that which was bestowed upon the Greek when the incarnate Son of God selected it to be the vehicle of the highest truth to the human race. The Christ could have come at any time and could, unquestionably, have spoken any language. It can not be regarded an accident that he came when he did, and that he chose to convey from himself and those whom he inspired the gospel of eternal life to all succeeding ages in the noble language of the Greeks.

There are, doubtless, reasons too numerous and profound to be elaborated here, why the Greek should have been selected, above all other languages, to embalm forever God's last and most precious words to the sons of men.

It can scarcely be regarded as partiality or

exaggeration to say that no language ever surpassed, if any ever equaled, the Greek in simplicity, in strength, in comprehensiveness, and in spirituality of expression. As no people ever excelled the Greeks in depth and precision of thought, so no language ever excelled theirs in clearness, fulness, and power. The Greek, too, was among the most flexible and musical of tongues, admitting a great variety of changes, both in the forms and in the order of its words, for reasons purely euphonic; so that its utterance might not tire the reader, the speaker, or the hearer.

We may get much help even in reading our English Bible with propriety by studying the Greek. Who has not felt the difficulty of giving the proper emphasis to the personal pronouns in reading the Bible? Now, in the Greek, when the pronoun is unemphatic it is never expressed, but is implied in the form of the verb; hence, whenever it is expressed in the Greek, it is more or less emphatic in the English, and should be made so to appear in the reading.

The Greek verb expressed every conceivable form and relation of action, being, and suffering with a greater variety of moods and tenses than any other ancient language; while its article, employed with noun, pronoun, verb, participle, adjective, adverb, and alone, helped to furnish the writer or the speaker of Greek with an instrument of thought and of expression which, for the perfect service of every mental power and the adequate portrayal of every mental process, was perhaps never equaled by any other language of earth. When Homer pictures the actions and passions of men in immortal verse; when Socrates, Plato, and Aristotle moralize and philosophize with almost surperhuman beauty and depth of conception; when Æschilus, Euripides, and Sophocles transcend the sons of men in poetic grandeur of thought and in entrancing richness of expression; when Xenophon details with simple elegance the story of some common events in a style of everlasting charm to men; or when Demosthenes riddles the crown intended for Æschines with words before bullets were in use, and keeps Philip and his army at bay by the thunder of his eloquence before cannon were invented, we are convinced that if the gods would talk with mortals they would use no other language than the Greek.

The discovery of the Rosetta Stone by Boussard, near the mouth of the Nile, in 1799, though apparently an accident, proved to be one of the most important events in the history of letters. It was the means of discovering to modern understandings the meaning of the records of the most ancient nations, especially of the Egyptians, and also of conferring upon the Greek language the distinguished honor of furnishing the key by which a great storehouse of mysteries was to be unlocked.

This stone contained three inscriptions, each in a tongue differing from the others; one in the ancient hieroglyphic or priestly style, one in the demotic or people's style, and one in Greek. No man then living could read either of the first two; but the Greek was found to be a translation of the other two, and so became the means of interpreting not only those two inscriptions, but also all other hieroglyphic and demotic records then known and that might be discovered to the end of time. Thus, with one hand the Greek has brought to the moderns the lost treasures of ancient lore, and with the other she brings God's highest message to men, his holy Word, of which she must forever remain the primal conservator for all who would receive it in the form indited by the Holy Ghost.

The Septuagint is a translation of the Old Testament into Greek, made perhaps (for its origin is quite obscure) about three hundred years before Christ. It is an invaluable treasure, giving us an interpretation of the Old Testament by competent Greek scholars at a very early day. It is a very significant fact that quotations from the Old Testament in the New are almost invariably taken from the Septuagint. Christ and his apostles quoted from it, and thereby sanctioned it. For several centuries after Christ it was read in the synagogues, the early Church regarding it as of equal authority and inspiration with the Hebrew text. The Greek Church so regards it to this day. Thus the Greek language brings to us even the Old Testament in semi-original and divinely sanctioned form, so that one who knows Greek may read the entire Bible in that most sacred tongue.

On some passages this version throws a very helpful light; as, when it is said that God hardened Pharaoh's heart, and, in the same connection, that Pharaoh hardened his own heart, the Greek uses different words for God's agency and for that of Pharaoh. When Pharaoh, Βαρυνεί, presses himself against God, God, Σκλαρυνεί, indurates or hardens Pharaoh's heart.

The multitude of those whose lack of education would forbid them to express an opinion on the subject have long opposed and decried the teaching of the Greek and Latin classics in our schools and colleges, and recently a few whose culture should entitle their opinions to respect have condemned the pur-

suit of these studies as a useless waste of time
and labor; but the great majority of scholars
have continued to maintain their utility and
to insist on their retention in every course of
liberal education.

How any one at all familiar with the terminology of the sciences can fail to appreciate
a knowledge of Greek is difficult to understand.
Such words as "physician," "botany," "telegraph," "telephone," "photograph," "optics,"
"acoustics," "electricity," "oxygen," and
thousands of others show the Greek origin of
the forms in which the wisest minds of the
ages have chosen to fix and transmit the treasures of knowledge. The sum of all we know
or may discover on the most important of all
subjects is expressed in the single Greek de-
rivative, *theology;* while he who was God
manifest in the flesh, though born a Hebrew,
and in that language appropriately called *Im-
manuel,* was yet to be known and preached
and worshiped through all ages under his
Greek name, *Jesus,* Saviour, (Ιησους, *healer*);
and this "his name shall endure forever,"

signifying his power to save (heal) his people from their sins.

The indebtedness of the English language to the Greek for a very large number of most beautiful and expressive words is so great that only ignorance can underestimate it. By far the greater part of the technical terminology of all the sciences is composed of derivatives or transfers from the Latin and the Greek. As illustrating the copiousness of our drafts upon Greek for means of fluent expression in English we note that all the more than fifteen hundred words in our language beginning with "*hy*" (with possibly a few exceptions) are derived from the Greek, and that every one of the almost five hundred words in our dictionaries beginning with "*hydr*" is derived from the single Greek word ὕδωρ, signifying water.

Several of the preceding remarks are applicable to the study of Greek in general; we come now to emphasize the importance of studying the Greek Testament in particular. He who would thoroughly know the mind of

8

a writer must study the words which he has employed. Here are writings professing to reveal truths hitherto unknown. The words are Greek, and he who would fully catch their thought and feel their force must surely know the Greek. The primal form of linguistic expression is as the die that prints the truth upon the soul of the reader. No translation can be supposed to equal the original, unless we are to expect translators to be inspired, as were the amanuenses of the Holy Ghost. There is something in the *very words* of him who spake as never man spake which no humanly devised forms can ever perfectly reproduce. The Divine Spirit we know enabled men to speak all the languages of earth (as on the day of Pentecost), yet God chose to give his gospel to men in Greek. The Latin was at this time more extensively used and was spoken by the dominant nations of the earth. Yet the Holy Ghost, the master of all languages, selected the Greek, in which to fix and preserve God's everlasting covenant with men. But whatever may have been the reasons for putting the

New Testament into Greek, the great question with us is: How may we best reach and realize the full power of its divine teaching? The apostle Paul declares that "all Scripture is given by inspiration of God,"* and Peter affirms that "holy men of God spake as they were moved by the Holy Ghost," † and that the prophecies of old came not by the will or wish of any man. Paul, in writing to the Corinthians, is more explicit still, assuring us that not only the matter, but also the words of his divine message were taught him by the Lord: "Which things also we speak, not in the words which man's wisdom teacheth, but which the Holy Ghost teacheth." ‡

Since the apostle affirms that spiritual truth is conveyed in spiritual words, can we doubt the importance of studying the words if we would get the mind of the Spirit? There are forms of expression and turns of thought of which

* 2 Timothy iii. 16.

† 2 Peter i. 21.

‡ 1 Corinthians ii. 12, 13.

no translation can adequately convey the force. The collocation of the words and the emphasis required by the style often add great force to a passage read in the original Greek. A translation can possibly give but a single view of the thought of a text, while he who studies the original may derive multiplied impressions of increasing strength and beauty, as one who beholds a landscape with leisurely and protracted gaze. Each Greek word is usually rendered by a single English equivalent, but the reader of the Greek itself may have his conceptions of the meaning of a passage deepened, varied, and enriched by the occurrence to his mind of half a dozen meanings of certain Greek words. The full force of this argument can be realized only by experiment. To know the joy of seeing one must see. One must read the New Testament in Greek to know the benefit of so doing. He who would know the thoughts of God most accurately must carefully study the words in which God has written his thoughts. Water brought in a vessel may be far better than no water at all, but must ever be inferior to that drunk from the fountain itself.

The labor required to familiarize oneself with the Greek will be amply repaid by its fruits. All Christians would be the better for the ability to read the New Testament in Greek, but every one who is to feed the flock of Christ as a minister of the word of life should surely be most anxious to learn all that the original text would impart to a competent and studious reader. He should be able to draw the sincere milk of the word from the mother's breast, and not be compelled to take a substitute from a bottle. A translation is a photograph; the original is the living man. Reading a translation is like looking at a cold and unchangeable painting; studying the original is like the satisfying contemplation of a landscape, whose varied richness and inexhaustible beauties are measured only by the penetrating power of the mind that beholds it.

He who reads a translation stands at the door of the mansion, waiting to greet any who may be sent out; he who reads the original enters within and cultivates, at his pleasure, the acquaintance of the inmates of the royal palace of truth. Some of the advantages of studying the original are obvious; others are as elusive as the operations of the spirit that constitutes the essence of a word. Remember that the Master said: "The words that I speak unto you, they are spirit and they are life."

We here introduce a few illustrations of the suggestions to be gotten by studying the Greek texts: "If any man *will do* his will," etc. The Greek is θέλῃ ποιεῖν, which means *desires, wishes,* or *is willing to do* his will. "The goodman of the house." Οἰκοδεσπότης simply *master,* neither *good,* as is implied in *good*man, nor *bad,* as might be inferred from our word *despot* derived from the latter part of the Greek compound.

"Add to your faith *virtue;*" Greek, ἀρετήν, *courage.*

"A *cheerful* giver, ἱλαρόν. simply *cheerful* or *willing.* The Greek does not precisely correspond in meaning with the English word *hilarious,* derived from it.

"Godliness." Not *God-like-ness*, but Εὐσέβεια, *reverence*, profound *adoration* toward God.

"Anathema." A thing accursed or devoted to destruction. "Maran atha"—"Our Lord cometh." The words are Syriac. "Conversation" —Ἀναστροφή—*conduct*, is never confined to the idea of words as it is in present usage.

"Slew all the children," τοὺς παιδὰς, *male* children. "Strain *at* a gnat;" strain *out* a gnat, διϋλίζω. "*Quick* and powerful"—*i. e., alive* and full of energy, ζῶν. Misled by this English word, a writer recently published a long article in a newspaper to prove that we should expect sudden or instantaneous results from God's word.

"The ax is *laid unto* the root of the trees"— *i. e., lies at*, κεῖται. "For it was *not* the time of figs." Let the smooth breathing of the οὐ be changed into the rough breathing, and it becomes οὑ, and the passage may be translated, *when indeed* it was the time of figs. This conjecture of my own, if allowable, certainly throws light on a very mysterious passage of scripture.

"Easily besetting sin,"—rather, *close-fitting garment*, ἱμάτιον for ἁμαρτίαν.

Should secular schools ever exclude the Greek from their courses of instruction, which they are not likely to do, Christian schools can never follow such an example. Christian scholars must ever delight in studying the New Testament in the Greek, and the word of our God in that divinely selected tongue must forever remain the sacred classic of the Church. To abandon the Greek would be to forsake the only standard by which the hundreds of translations into the various languages, dialects, and idioms of earth can be verified, harmonized, and authenticated as the word of God. Let us study—study Greek, that we may be able thoroughly to understand and rightly to teach the word of God. The time has passed, if it ever existed, when sanctified ignorance in a public teacher could even seem to be edifying to men; and it certainly can no longer be acceptable to God, when he has placed the means of knowledge within the reach of every student. Let us search the sacred Book in the original Greek, as for hid treasure; and familiarize ourselves with the very words which the Spirit used, that we may be filled with the spirit which they convey.

We need not only preachers and teachers whose hearts are aflame with the fire caught from the living words of the Master, but we need also profound expositors and learned exegetes who can meet the enemy in the gate and reprove the ignorance, the presumption, or the gracelessness of those advocates of higher (or lower) criticism who would rob mankind of the water of life by picking holes in every vessel in which it is carried.

THE SOUL'S PRAYER.

Father, I ask one gift of thee,
Deny not that one gift to me,
Thy giving can not waste thy store,
Nor can withholding make it more.

Since thou dost give and not upbraid,
Thy suppliant need not be afraid;
Thy riches all are to be given—
Thou wilt not e'en deny us heaven.

I need not tell thee my request,
For thou canst read it in my breast;
Grant me, I pray, the unspoken boon,
Turn thou my midnight into noon.

Make me, O Lord, what I should be,
And give me all thou hast for me;
The fulness of thy nature give,
That I henceforth in thee may live.

The night is gone, the death is past,
My soul finds life in thee at last;
Infinite joy thou givest me,
Infinite praise I'd give to thee!

A slave to sin, I lingered long,
Salvation now is all my song!
My soul, exulting in my Lord,
Finds all her prayer in Christ is heard.

WE MISS OUR FATHER EVERYWHERE.*

We miss him in the corner where
Now vacant sits the old armchair,
We miss him when the meal is spread,
We miss him when the grace is said,
We miss him at the hour of prayer,
We miss our Father everywhere.

The world looks now no more the same,
Its bright things all seem cold and tame,
Its gladness mocks our lonely woe,
And taunts our grief where'er we go;
No sound is sweet, no scene is fair,
We miss our Father everywhere.

I miss him on my morning walk
I miss his wise, observant talk;
At evening hour I walk alone,
Since he who walked with me is gone;
The fields and woods are sad and bare—
I miss my Father everywhere.

In vain we search for him we've lost,
We can not pass the stream he's crossed;
But while our hearts throb out his name

---

*Written upon the death of my father, Dr. J. E. P. Hunnicutt, who died at Turin, Ga., March 7, 1884.

We hear a kindly voice proclaim:
" Weep not my children, God is near;
A home of peace awaits you here."

Then light the fire when day's work's through
As Father long was wont to do,
And let its glow the orphans cheer
When they at eve shall gather near;
His spirit, too, shall join with ours,
Communing there with heavenly powers.

Around the home-hearth still we'll meet
And seek for strength at Jesus' feet,
There wiping oft affection's tears
New hope shall spring for future years;
There we shall prove the power of prayer—
Our Father's God will still be there.

NOISE AS A BRAIN-DEVELOPER.

LITTLE had I suspected, till recently, that while the propensity to "make a noise in the world" is characteristic of most energetic men, the noise-making of all healthy children is not only natural, but is perhaps physically necessary to the highest development of their brains. Every child is instinctively a noise-maker, and my theory is that certain kinds of noise are powerfully promotive of brain-growth. The voice, the ear, and the brain are by no means independent of each other; but vocal chords, auricular structure, and high-wrought brain for thought are all joined in special and mutual helpfulness.

Human life, with reference to our inquiry, may be divided into three periods: (1) the period of uproarious noise-making; (2) the period of silent work; (3) the period of still-ness and decadence. In the first, the child lives in ceaseless noise and perpetual motion; in the second, man studies, works, and attends to business, avoiding noise and utilizing motion; in the third, both noise and motion lose their charms, and stillness is courted, while enfeebling age lulls man to his final sleep.

Men are so constituted that all their powers can not be equally active at the same time; some must rest while others work. The chief function of a child is to grow. The entire body, including the brain, should grow rapidly in childhood. One great promoter of growth is motion. Chemical decomposition and recomposition of particles, adjustment of molecular elements, enlargement and increase of strength in all parts of the body are the result of activity. And what motion is to the body in general, sound is to the brain in particular, the brain being precluded by its surroundings from the effects of motion on other parts of the body. It can scarcely be questioned that the exercise of each and all of the five bodily senses has a great effect in developing the capacities of the brain for its varied kinds of work. The impinging of light upon the eye affects the brain through the optic nerve. The contact and movement of sand upon the tender skin of a child produces not only exquisite pleasure through the sense of touch, but also a quickening of perceptivity and of general bodily consciousness. All children should have sand beds to play in.

That the exercise of the sense of hearing is essentially connected with the higher powers of the brain may be inferred from the fact that the auditory ganglia of the brain are developed along with and usually in proportion to the intelligence of the animal. In the codfish, for instance, the optic and olfactory ganglia are distinctly shown, with the cerebral lobes and the cerebellum; while here, as in most reptiles and even in rabbits and birds, the auditory ganglia are almost rudimentary. Indeed, the marvelously complex apparatus of the sense of hearing in the higher animals seems to demonstrate the eminent importance of the power of hearing to the functions of the brain.

The effect of mere sound, regardless of its significance, would be to develop the brain not so much in size as in molecular structure and in functional capacity, as the seat of sensations and the author of movements. This I hold to be the easiest possible mode of enhancing the thinking power of the brain. Should a child strongly exert his mental powers in order to increase the thinking capacity of his brain, he would thereby in large degree suspend the normal activity of parts of his body, restrict growth, and injure his health; as may be seen in the case of young children who are excessively fond of study or are too much pressed to books. Noise exercises the brain without tiring it, as play does the body. The inrush of sound through the auditory apparatus to the brain quickens and enhances its powers, as play does those of the body.

It is said that no two particles of matter are in actual contact. Perhaps those of the best brains come nearest to touching that they may present the highest possible degree of vibratility. The effect of multitudinous vocal sounds, to which no attention is paid, seems to be to promote such an adjustment of the particles of the brain as shall qualify it for higher grades of intellectual work and for the authorship of more graceful muscular movements. Sound-waves from without and heart-pulses from within conspire to promote that exquisite vibratility in the millionary gossamers of the brain which make it the inscrutable mystery of science, the miracle of miracles among the works of God.

The scientific theory of sound lends itself readily to the confirmation of these views. While waves of light are transverse, waves of sound are longitudinal—*i. e.*, in the direction of the motion of the wave. Hence, waves of sound would be eminently calculated to affect decidedly the delicate matter of the brain by means of the impulses which would reach it through the ear. And does not the brain respond to the contributions which sounds have made to its thinking capacity by fabri-

9

cating its very thoughts in sounds? Does not consciousness reveal the fact that we not only think in words, but that the mind formulates those words to itself, in their last physical analysis, in *mere sounds?* Repeat mentally a familiar passage of literature, and you have no vision of the shapes or numbers of the letters or words, but the mind runs through the series of appropriate sounds whereby the thought is expressed. Do we not, then, think in sounds? The truth of this theory would demand not only appropriate noise, but good hearing organs in order to the highest intellectuality. And do we not find the congenitally deaf not only dumb, but much restricted in their mental capacities? Would not children of good hearing be greatly lessened in mental activity if reared in silence?

But we need not now invade the realms of the anatomist or of the metaphysician. We may confidently expect future investigations to show that certain meaningless sounds impinging on the matter of the brain exert a powerful effect upon the intellectuality of man.

Let us rather look at the phenomena of childhood, as a period of noise-making, comparing
it with the same period in the lives of brutes.
Who ever knew the command, "Stop your
noise, children?" to fail to kill all the joy of
the rompers, if it did not stop the play
altogether? To forbid the motions and the
noises of children is to suppress the fountains of vitality within them. Yet noise is
no essential part of play. It is only intellectual, human young that must play noisily, or
not at all. The young of almost all lower
animals play, but they play for the most part
silently. This silence in the young of wild
animals may be accounted for by the instinct
of self-preservation, lest noise should betray
them to their foes. But this reason will not
account for the noiseless sports of the young
of domestic animals. Lambs, kids, colts, and
calves evidently enjoy their noiseless play,
and puppies at times give only slight pre-
monitions that they will be loud barkers
some day, by their half-suppressed guttural
laugh-grunts in play.

The young of birds seem too much taken up with the work of digestion while full-fed during the growing period, or with the pangs of hunger when starved to lighten them for flight as they approach maturity, to think much about play. The cries of the nestling, which, by revealing its whereabouts, have brought death to many a hapless birdling, have in them nothing of the gladness of play. Only the child, the prince among animals, free, fearless, and divinely intellectual, is pre-eminently a noise-maker in all his play; insomuch that we may say, the more noise he makes the happier he is, and—may we not add?—the more intellectual he becomes.

But this propensity to stir the aerial ocean round into a dinning tempest of sound in order to their highest satisfaction, though peculiar to the human species, is not confined to little children. College boys, when at liberty, are notoriously vociferous except when engaged in schemes whose execution demands the secrecy of silence. College "cries" are becoming more and more universal and uproarious as intellectuality advances. When the sentimental collegian saws with his fiddle bow through hours wearisome to all but himself, he is doubtless wearing off the rugosities of his cranial convolutions, preparatory to the due realization and expression of the tenderer affections of his heart. Those sandpapering sounds adjust his brain to the softer emotions of his soul, and he is a different man forever after.

This universal propensity to noise-making can not be regarded as an accident, much less as an expression of a vicious desire to surprise, annoy, or alarm others. It doubtless finds its deep and sufficient explanation in the physiology of the brain.

Those schools, perhaps they should be styled scholastic prisons, where too much stillness is required and too much silence is exacted of the growing child have often produced effects the very opposite of those intended by parents and teachers, and have tended rather to make dull machines than lively thinkers; while, perhaps, loud-studying schools have made up in general brain-de-velopment what they lacked in special and technical mind-training. Even a blow upon the ear, not severe enough to injure the organ internally, has, in possible instances, produced far better effects upon the brain than the temper of the administrator would allow to be expected upon the heart of the child. If children do not live by noise, it is largely by noise they prove they are alive. Scotch law declares that if a child does not cry loud enough to be heard it is never alive at all.

While I was writing this essay three of the prettiest little girls marched unceremoniously into my study, each holding one of McGinty's babies in her hand,

And they blew and they blew and they blew till
I found all my protests were utterly futile.

What could I do, but rejoice in their joy, recognize the happy and unexpected demonstration of my theory, and congratulate the parents on the infallible promise of intel-

lectuality in their children? From this view
of the question it should be expected that
noisy children would excel in manifestations
of mental power. And who can say they do
not? Are not the children of negroes, of Indians, and of all other unintellectual races by
far less noisy in play and elsewhere than the
children of the Caucasian race? The former
often in their frolics remind one of the mute
dulness of young brutes.

How much to be regretted it is that all the
sore-nerved mothers and thousands of others
who through the ages have been afflicted and
tormented by the ever-varying, never-ceasing,
and irrepressible babblings, rompings, roar-
ings, and thunderings of playing children
did not know that all these noises were not
only proofs, presages, and promoters of high
intellectuality, but were really essential agents
in producing the greatest minds of the world!
Only think, that all the bawlings of all the
bawlers that ever bawled were eminently promotive of mind-growth in the bawlers! The
very thought is a balm to the ears of adult

humanity, and turns millionary torments into
joys.

> Then let the children loudly play
> And every bawler have his day.
> The bawling thrills the brain within,
> And thought-power grows amid the din.

THE WEATHER AND I.

THE weather and I could never agree;
Just why this was so, I never could see,
1 When the weather was dry I wished it would rain,*
And when it was warm I clamored for cool—
To quarrel with him was simply my rule.

I warred with the weather for many long years,
I found fault with him and he pinched my ears;
2 Now why should the weather afflict us with pain?
'Twas always the wrong sort of weather for me—
My habit forever his wrong side to see.

So, when I was pleased, and when I was not,
The weather kept changing from cold back to hot;
3 An unruly fellow he surely must be!
I cowered before his on-sweeping blast,
And found I was under the weather at last.

Oh, then, I bethought me, with him I'll agree,
And the wisdom of all his changes I'll see—
4 Since I can't make him submissive to me;
In sunshine or showers, hot or cold, I will say,
What beautiful weather! a very fine day!

---

* The numbered lines may be read as a stanza.

How gladsome the sunshine! how sweet are the
  showers!
The heat and the cold are the heavenly powers;
5 O shame that I ever found fault with my friends!
  They fill all the earth with fruits and with flow-
    ers,
  And show us God's thoughts, far higher than
    ours.

Shall I ever again of the weather complain?
The worst-seeming days are good in the main;
6 Could I make them better for God's gracious ends?
  Each day is the best that could possibly be,
  To those who have eyes its blessings to see.

A SATIRE ON UNBELIEF.

THE world thus far has banked on truth,
As well became its artless youth;
But now she feels that she's grown wise,
And boldly proves the power of lies.
A fiction's been for centuries told
Of Eve's and Adam's sin of old,
How they transgressed the rule of heaven
And forth were from the garden driven;
Of how they fell from God's good grace,
And sank the souls of all their race.
Long after that, we hear it said,
A covenant was with Abraham made
By which he was to serve the Lord,
And God was pledged to be his God,
And all his seed were to be blessed,
And all the earth should be possessed
By one descended from his line
Who should with heavenly virtues shine.
So, when the years had rolled away,
The writers of this story say,
A child was born, a wondrous child,
On whom a virgin mother smiled,

King of the Jews and God's own Son,
Jesus, the Christ, the Holy One,
Who brought a gracious plan from heaven
By which men's sins might be forgiven.
He taught and wrought and died to save,
And conquered sin, hell, and the grave;
He claimed the world as all his own,
And said its praise his name should crown.
His followers say he went to heaven
Till what he taught the world should leaven.
Science now late her head exalts
Proclaiming all this story false.
The supernatural can't be true,
'Twould all the fixed laws undo.
Yet Jesus' doctrines widely spread,
They're to the souls of men as bread;
Wise men say they can not doubt them—
They could not live or die without them;
Honor and truth spring from their sway,
Our thoughts are shaped by them to-day.
Obeying them all lives are blest,
Of moral fruits they yield the best,
From strength to strength their votaries go,
Bounds to their empire none may know.
Jesus is worshiped everywhere,
His name gives form to every prayer,
All those who follow him do right,
As guided by unearthly light,

While love and joy and all good will
The lives of his disciples fill.
Yea, strange to tell, we see this day
He holds the world beneath his sway.
The years are numbered from his birth,
And Christians rule the spacious earth,
The nations that confess him Lord
Could sweep the world of Satan's horde.
If lies thus take earth's ills away
Then may these lies forever stay.
How strange is this, could truth do more—
The truth that infidels adore?

THE FORMER DAYS AND THESE.

"SAY not thou, What is the cause that the former days were better than these? for thou dost not inquire wisely concerning this." (Eccl. vii. 10.) Had Solomon written nothing more than this weighty warning against forming erroneous opinions on a question which through the ages involves alike the honor of God and the welfare of man, he would deserve a place among the wisest of our race.

Were the former days really better than these, or do they only seem so? Our object in this essay will be to show how and why, even though they were not better, there will ever be a tendency in many minds to think that they were, and yet that the evidence is decidedly in favor of the present when compared with the past.

Among those especially who have passed

the meridian of life, the opinion is apt to prevail that whatever pertains to the welfare of man is on the decline. The seasons appear to them to be growing more severe, the heat more intense, the cold more intolerable, while all malignant elements combine in unwonted ways to ruin our peace. To them, every form of evil seems to be on the increase, and the good to be everywhere pushed to the wall. The situation is sad and the prospect gloomy. If the world is not really on the "easy descent to hell," it is honestly feared by many that it is nearly approaching the verge of that perilous declivity. The sadness of those who view things thus is intensified by the thought of the past. "The former days were better than these," say they. "Give us back the good old days, or we must go down in sorrow to our graves." How far such views and feelings as these, affecting as they do thousands of the best people, are warranted by facts, and how far they result from the conditions and operations of their own minds, is a question well worthy of investigation.

In what respects, then, is it thought that the former days were better? Surely none believe that the past had any advantage over the present in the useful arts or in the practical sciences. Within the present century new applications of steam as a motive power have revolutionized the manufacturing and commercial operations of the world, increasing beyond all anticipation the physical comforts and enjoyments of life, and wonderfully facilitating transportation and rapid and extensive intercommunication among men. The use of gas and of electricity as illuminators has furnished guiding and protecting light to thousands of cities that had previously been accustomed to sit in dangerous darkness when sun and moon were out of sight. Electricity has been made to run on obedient errands over lines constructed and located with marvelous skill and enterprise, bearing and delivering messages of thought to the most distant parts of the world with such speed and accuracy as to almost annihilate space, and amazingly transcending all previous conception of possibility. The government of a nation, located at its capital, whence diverging and ramifying telegraphic wires spread like network over its surrounding domains, may constitute itself a grand sensorium, almost as quickly conscious as a human brain of any important change in even the most distant part of the body politic. As a motive power it works like a magician, and is superseding even steam itself as a mover of the machinery of the world.

Astronomers have pushed their inquiries into distant space, discovering new worlds and systems of worlds; have given special attention to the sun, and by the aid of the spectroscope have been enabled to read a revelation of the elementary constituents of the great king of day written by his own beams. Geologists, too, have been searching the depths of the earth and are beginning to read the chronicles of creation that have been buried, but not lost, for uncalculated ages, from leaves of the great earth-volume that had never been turned before.

10

Indeed, in all knowledge we have been progressing, and Mr. Edison, the wizard of the nineteenth century, is almost daily surprising the world by some invention or discovery in the realm of science.

Neither in the extent and variety of learning, nor in its skilful application to the purposes of life, is the present age inferior to any that preceded it. Wherein, then, is the world thought to be retrograding? In moral status in the power and prevalence of truth and righteousness, we are told. The preaching is not so powerful nor the singing so inspiring as they once were. People are neither so good nor so happy as they were in former years. Men are lapsing from the faith of their fathers and losing confidence in the teachings of the Bible, while diabolical wickedness of many kinds prevails. We have fallen upon evil times.

Are these really facts? We have two sources of evidence, history and experience. The testimony of history is neither meager nor doubtful. Universal tradition corroborates

the brief Biblical account of a flood by which
the Almighty swept from the earth a vast
population whose wickedness had become intolerable, thereby not only preventing the
further increase of their ungodliness, but forever hiding from the generations to come all
special knowledge of a people the particulars
of whose history would have been an ever-
recurring suggestion to sin. Notwithstanding
this, wickedness of the grossest kind became
shockingly prevalent among all nations previous to the coming of Christ. Earthquakes,
famines, and pestilences were penalties which
demonstrated the enormity of men's crimes.
Pharaoh, Sodom, Korah, and many others
evidence a degree of criminality as then prevalent of which we can now form no adequate
conception.

The political history of the world for many
centuries is little else than an account of the
animosities, strifes, and murders of rival prin-
ces; the oppression or enslavement of their
subjects, and the wholesale destruction of
their enemies. More men, in proportion to

the population, often lost their lives by private feuds or public wars then, in a few years, than now perish from the same causes in a century. Social and personal morals were exceedingly depraved. Woman was universally enslaved and abused by the brutal power of tyrannical man; children in some of the most enlightened nations were taught to steal; revolting scenes of bloodshed and horror were everywhere regarded as the most delightful entertainments for all sexes and classes of society; while the hope of drinking their enemies' blood from bowls made of their skulls was their very highest idea of felicity in the world to come.

But lest we be thought to draw our evidence from too remote a period, let us look at the state of the world after the more general spread of the gospel. It is true the picture seems somewhat modified, yet it is sufficiently dark. Wars and manifold wickednesses claim a large share of attention. Even the Church of Christ becomes often involved in such bloody struggles with heretics or heathen that we might reasonably infer that it was her chief aim to destroy, instead of to save, men's lives. It is scarcely a hundred years since the Christian world arrived at the conclusion that persecution of heretics was not the noblest mark of the divinity of the Church. The dark ages—dark not only in literature, but in morals—spread their gloomy centuries like a wall of blackness between us and the apostles' day; centuries which surely no sane man could wish to have repeated in the world's history. But during the last few centuries new and powerful agencies for good have been abroad. The invention of the art of printing has greatly facilitated the multiplication and lessened the cost of copies of the Holy Scriptures, and the Bible, released from the thraldom of concealment in which it had lain for ages, has gone forth a radiant luminary into the kingdoms of darkness and the nations have been quickened and blessed by its heavenly light.

The invention of railroads has greatly facilitated all kinds of transportation, men have mingled with each other, knowledge of every kind has greatly increased, and civilized man

seems to have been advancing in wisdom and
virtue.   He who judges the course of a stream
by objects circling in eddies along its banks
would be apt to mistake the direction of the
current.   The battle between good and evil
should be judged by the movements of nations
and the moral trend of the centuries.   Let us
note a few signs:

1. From the time when Constantine marched
to victory under the banner of the cross, Christianity has deepened and widened her power
till Christian nations have now become the
dominant nations of the world.

2. Multiplying millions are being annually
expended in Christian charities, churches,
schools, hospitals, and asylums; all governments are being mitigated, and prison discipline is everywhere being humanized, through
the influence of the name of Christ.

3. The spirit and practise of war are greatly
diminished.   With the amazing increase in
means of transportation, which might have
multiplied wars and intensified conflicts, nations have learned forbearance, which is evi-

denced by the numerous arbitrations of national disputes and the urgent proposal of treaties of universal and permanent arbitration between all nations.

4. Never before did Christians make such efforts to save the heathen as are now being made. Certainly one of the most marked features of the latter half of the nineteenth century is its missionary feature.

5. Among the greatest obstacles to the progress of Christianity have been the schisms and strifes among its professors. The failure of the Church to keep herself pure and peaceable hindered her spread more than all opposition from without. The errors, corruptions, and tyranny of Romanism gave rise to Protestantism. Limitation of mind and selfishness of heart gave ignorance and ambition a devilish sway in the Church, till even the heathen rejected the caricature of Christianity as a substitute for the powerless rites of their ancestral religions. But now we see the day---not of perfect harmony, but of milder strife—when Churches contend less for dogma and more

for Christ, less for victory and more for the salvation of souls. Surely the Church of to-day presents less of the repulsive and more of the attractive and convincing before the eyes of the unbelieving world than did the Church of two or five hundred years ago.

Thus we perceive that a general survey of the past forces upon us the conclusion that the world has not been moving backward. There may have been temporary periods of exception, but the general tendency and movement have been from bad to good, from darkness unto light.

Indeed, we are ever liable to learn less than the truth concerning the evils of the past. The natural preference of the mind for good rather than evil; the injunction of the classic motto, "Nothing concerning the dead unless it be good;" and the natural tendency of men to speak favorably of their own achievements and characters—authorize us to expect history to give us a somewhat flattering picture of the past. The bearer of evil tidings can give no pleasure by his tale, but is liable to be regarded as was the man who ran to tell David of Absalom's death. The historian often looks through friendship's partial eyes or charity's fault-hiding evil. It is hard to learn the whole truth about the past. History is apt to show it

With mentioned faults a little dwarfed,
  And many faults untold.

But perhaps we have misconceived the position of those with whom we would reason. They do not mean to say that ancient were better than modern times, but that during the period of their experience the times have certainly not improved; and they sigh for the "good old days." The world, the Church, and all things seemed to them better a few decades ago than now. The children were more obedient and respectful, the parents more discreet and careful, the preachers were more pious and profound, the laws were better executed, and even the water they drank from grandfather's spring was colder and sweeter than any the earth affords in these degenerate days.

There is something so natural and at the same time so saddening in this state of mind that its philosophy well deserves our investigation. Let us examine it. Were the bygone days which we hear so much eulogized really superior to these in which we live, or do they only seem so? We think the superiority of the past is only seeming. How, then, does this seeming become a most affecting reality to many wise people who would not be unjustly censorious of the times in which they live?

1. A poet tells us:

'Tis distance lends enchantment to the view.
And clothes the mountain in its azure hue.

Doubtless the appearance of other matters than mountains often depends upon the distance of time as well as of territory over which they are viewed. Were we nearer to those distant days, they would not seem the same to us. A closer inspection would reveal many deformities not perceived in the distance, even as a mountain range, which looks when seen afar soft and smooth as the sky, becomes, on a near approach, a rough and craggy barren, quite unlovely to behold.

2. The source of this error may be the better appreciated by bearing in mind the fact that memory instinctively retains that which is good, and as naturally rejects that which is evil. The mind treasures the remembrance of all things good and pleasant as a constant source of joy. Though duty and necessity often conspire to produce a habit of dwelling upon the evils of the present, collecting their evidences and brooding over their effects, interest and pleasure incline us to forget the evil of the past and remember the good. The oft-recurring vexations and disappointments of the present drive the mind to seek solace amid the delights which memory has sagaciously stored away in her treasury. The fresh scratch of a brier upon our person produces more present dissatisfaction than the cicatrix of a dangerous wound which has long since healed. The petty annoyances of a single day of ordinary life are more trying to even a patient spirit than are the remembered horrors of a score of hard-fought battles. There is a sort of joy in the recollection of

ills that are past, arising no doubt from the thought that we have escaped from them and are beyond their reach; but the instinct of self-preservation disposes us to exaggerate every evil which affects us in the present. What a happy thing, too, is it that memory prefers to treasure up only good! Is it not a trace of the divine nature yet lingering in the soul, burying evil in forgetfulness and holding only to the good? Let us not be deceived; the past had its evils which are out of sight, the present has more of good perhaps than we are prepared to see.

3. The correctness of those views will the more clearly appear if we consider that for several reasons we almost necessarily give a disportionately large share of attention to present ills as compared with those that are past, while the reverse takes place with regard to whatever is good. A natural and often unconscious selfishness leads us to magnify the faults and vices of our cotemporaries; while personal rivalries, jealousies, and hates too frequently disqualify us for

forming a correct estimate of their virtues. Perfect impartiality is scarcely to be expected, however honestly aimed at by an interested party. Besides, our very nearness to the evils about us, by a well-known law of physical optics, not inapplicable to moral vision, renders it impossible that present ills should not occupy an unduly large part of our field of view, when compared with those of the distant past. A man's hand laid over his eyes shuts out the world. It may be asked: Does not the same law apply to our estimate of the favorable aspects of past and present, and will not the one error counterbalance the other? We answer negatively, since the dangerousness of the present evils must, for the time, distract our attention from all other objects of thought. A single source of imminent evil, however small, effectually prevents, while it occupies the mind, all consideration of a hundred sources of greater good. A violent storm of an hour's duration attracts more attention and leaves a more profound impression upon the minds of a community than a score of serene and sunshiny days. A single riot is more noticed than the preaching of a hundred sermons or the peaceful continuance of civil government for a twelvemonth. Self-preservation, or the shunning of all evil, is the strongest instinct of humanity. Hence the evils which affect *us now* are thought greater than all others.

4. That good men should find themselves often regretting the backward moral tendencies of the world is not surprising. Wicked men have no idea of sin except such as is suggested by its calamitous effects. But the Christian, in whose soul the principles of the divine nature have been developed, feels a constantly increasing sensitiveness to the moral turpitude of sin. The illuminated understanding, the quickened conscience, becomes painfully cognizant of whatever is inconsistent with the divine will. The more we become like God, the more keenly alive are we to all ungodliness. The world seems to be growing worse, because we are growing better; the regions around ap-

pear darker, because the light within us is increasing.

It was when Elijah was most zealous for God's kingdom that he believed himself to be its only surviving representative. His horror at the surrounding wickedness blinded him to the thousands who had not bowed the knee to Baal.

5. Let us not then infer the moral deterioration of the world from our own advancement in holiness; for as we grow in grace sin must ever continue to appear yet "yet more exceeding sinful;" and so the ungodly world seems always to be growing worse to those who are going on unto perfection. The train that is moving more slowly than ours seem to us to be moving backward.

6. But perhaps the saddest of all reasons for gloomy views of the present moral state and tendency of the world is to be found in the backslidden condition of those who entertain these views. How much of the appearance of any object seen is due to the mind that perceives is a question which philosophers

find not easy to answer. We know that the color of any object may be changed by throwing upon it in succession the different prismatic rays. We know, too, that certain diseased states of the brain or of the organs of vision result in the most absurd and distorted perceptions of sight. The notion we form of the moral state of society is perhaps quite as much dependent upon the condition of our own hearts as the appearance of physical things is upon the quality of the light or upon the condition of our visual organs. To the mourning spirit every object is suggestive of sadness, even the very same which to the cheerful heart is a minister of gladness. The soul that has lost the joys of former days sees all things through a tear-dimmed eye, sombered by the shadow which itself has cast.

Selfishness, too, powerfully aids the deception. Men are loath to believe others generally better than themselves. When a soul has wandered from the light of God's countenance and walks amid the fogs of doubt and unbelief, it sees all men enveloped in the insignia of its own unfaithfulness. Whoever knew one who had lost the joys of the great salvation that did not think that the Church and all the appliances and evidences of grace had manifestly deteriorated within the period of his remembrance?

We read of one in olden times whose feet were almost gone, whose steps had well-nigh slipped, and who had rashly concluded that the righteous have no advantage over the wicked, and that it is a vain thing to serve God. In the blindness of his mind he had begun to envy the apparent prosperity of the wicked. Having lost his own faith, he at once imagined all faith to be vain. But when he went to the sanctuary and studied God's truth in the light of his providence, he was overwhelmed with a sense of the folly of his reasoning and the wickedness of his thoughts.

It is a fortunate thing that all men are never sick at once, and we should beware of inferring the moral state of the world from the unhealthy, backslidden condition of individual souls.

11

7. But finally, the prevalency of the idea that the days of our early remembrance were better than these is attributable, more than to any other single cause, to the permanency of early impressions. There is a mysterious beauty in the relative states and operations of the mind at different periods of life. The intimate connection between the mental states of childhood and old age is one of the most curious facts of our earthly existence. It is at once interesting and wonderful to see the resurrection in the minds of the aged of the long-dormant impressions of early childhood. Our lives seem naturally divisible into three great periods: the period of feeling, the period of action, and the period of reflection or retrospection. As age advances the mind seems to look farther back into its early history, as if its final operations were but an unwinding of the thread of thought, and living childhood over again; or, as if life under some unseen power first flowed so far forth and then ebbed back to its starting-point. Hence it is that the aged are never in perfect sympathy

with current events, but are perpetually dwelling in the past.

"Still o'er those scenes their memory wakes,
And fondly broods with miser care;
Time but the impression stronger makes,
As streams their channels deeper wear."

Fortunately for the young and for the aged too, the mind's first impressions of its earthly home are of the most favorable character. To those just entering it, the world is full of beauty. To the young the sunshine is brighter, the breeze more delightful, the water more refreshing, fruits more delicious, and all scenery more delectable than to the old. To them all things wear the charm of novelty. With eager curiosity they go forth into life, their minds being rendered peculiarly receptive by the absence of all pre-occupying thoughts and anxious cares. With fervent and untutored imagination they exaggerate every object, viewing all things as colored by a glowing fancy and magnified by contrast with the diminutiveness of the beholder. Seeking happiness with an instinct as unerring as that which guides the butterfly to the sweets of the new-blown flower, they see and hear and taste all things beautiful and delightful. They neither know nor desire to know of the evils of life. It is only the experience of after-years that teaches them that many of the flowers that charmed their childhood were poisonous; that serpents often lie concealed beneath the fairest bowers; that our dearest friendships are of short duration and sometimes insincere; that labor and disappointment are the lot of all; that losses and diseases are inevitable attendants of life; and that death pursues us through every period of our earthly career with a thousand executioners, infallibly sure by one means or another to arrest us at last and hurry us away from all we here have loved. Those who judge the world by the impressions received in childhood always judge it amiss.

Comparing things seen through youth's admiring eyes with things as viewed through the penetrating vision of schooled, suspicious and often embittered age, it is not strange tha they should find their preference all in favor of the former days. The world was never so good as we once fancied it to be; it is better now than our chafed spirits are willing to admit.

Children are just as happy now as their grandparents were in their childhood seventy years ago. The world does not grow worse, though men grow old. The living majority is always young. No, we do not inquire wisely concerning this. God is better than our thoughts, and his kingdom is not failing.

Christians ripen in grace more rapidly than the world around them. Their moral progress is more speedy. Hence they become discouraged when viewing the apparently slow (and seemingly backward) moral movement of the ages.

Jacob's reply to Pharaoh is characteristic of the aged: "Few and evil have the days of the years of my life been, and have not attained unto the days of the years of the life of my fathers in the days of their pilgrimage." Not Benjamin alive nor all the glory of

Joseph in Egypt could even for a moment suspend Jacob's habit of dwelling upon the sorrows of his life. The absence of his beloved boys had burned lines of grief into his soul so deep that no present joy, however great, could suddenly obliterate them.

The habit of looking only into the past for models of perfection was the natural result of all efforts at improvement on the part of men to whom the future was wholly unrevealed. Hence the heathen statesmen, philosophers, and poets exhausted their skill in depicting the excellences of the primitive times, which they supposed to be in exact proportion to their remoteness, so that the earliest period could only be fitly represented as the *golden age* of the world. From that blissful state the world seemed to them to have perpetually declined by the gradual loss of every element of happiness. This heathenish idea has doubtless had much influence in producing a very general tendency in modern minds to exaggerate every desirable characteristic of the past, and to disparage every claim of excellence on the part of the present. Christianity first undertook to teach mankind that into the future, and not into the past, they should look for the highest types of perfection. Yet many fail to appreciate her doctrine and spend much time in vain regrets that the present is not as the past was, and in fruitless endeavors to recall the irrevocable, and live over the lives of their grandparents. The times have changed, and we have changed with them. We are not, and should not be, precisely what our ancestors were. It may be profitable to review the errors of the past, that we may avoid them; but to undertake or desire to repeat the history of the past is sheer folly. The world can not elevate and redeem itself by repeating its own history, Increasing age and experience reveal to men the existence of internal as well as external sources of evil of which they had no conception in early life; hence they sigh most naturally for the innocence of childhood. Conscious of the disease and ignorant alike of its cause and of its remedy, the restless spirit seeks relief in the happy remembrance of the innocence and peace of bygone earlier days.

That vain regrets for departed blessings and futile attempts to restore the world to the fancied status of some former period should have been perpetually repeated from age to age by men destitute of divine revelation is no surprising thing. The future being to them a dread obscurity, they could look only into the past for criteria by which to estimate the present. But for men accepting as inspired a book whose author saw and declared the future as clearly as the past, and whose pages are burdened with promises of things to come more glorious in all respects than the past has ever known, such idolatry of the past is as inconsistent with sound wisdom as it is with saving faith. We have no evidence that men were ever better satisfied with their surroundings than are the men of the present generation. Every past age was to those who lived in it a present period and no more satisfactory to them than our times are to us. The men of every past generation lived and

died regretting the unlikeness of their times
to the former times. The Christian revelation, on the contrary, abounds with promises
of future good. No state of personal or of
social life was ever so greatly blessed that
its successor was not legitimately expected
to surpass it. The world's advancement in
all real good is to be accomplished not by a
repetition of its own history, but by a perpetual approach to a state whose ideal is revealed only from heaven. The model is ever
above and before us.

The New Jerusalem is to come down from
God out of heaven. The angel's exhortation
to Lot, "Look not behind thee," embodies
the sentiment of heaven's instruction to the
men of every age. We are to "forget the
steps already trod and onward urge our way."
We are not to think of returning to Egypt,
as did some (and were not they the proto-
types of our modern eulogizers of the past?)
whose souls were married to memories of its
flesh-pots, but we are to look only to the un-
imagined delights of Canaan before us.

Does the kingdom of heaven among men seem to any to be waning? Let them remember that the stone which was cut out of the mountain without hands filled the whole earth, and that the promises of God are as sure as his power can make them. Though "I visit their transgressions with the rod, and their iniquity with stripes, nevertheless my loving-kindness will I not utterly take from him, nor suffer my faithfulness to fail." (Ps. lxxxix. 32, 33.)

"In the days of these kings shall the God of heaven set up a kingdom, which shall never be destroyed. . . . It shall stand forever." "Of the increase of his government and peace there shall be no end." Surely, if these predictions and promises are true and faithful, there can be no absolute deterioration in the world's moral state. Surely they are mistaken who suppose the world is growing worse, for some in every preceding age thought the same, and if they thought truly, then is the world nearer perdition now than ever before. But God, who is the strength of our hearts and our por-

tion forever, has assured us of better things.
"Many shall run to and fro, and knowledge
shall be increased." "The earth shall be full
of the knowledge of the Lord, as the waters
cover the sea." "The kingdoms of this world
are to become the kingdoms of our Lord, and
of his Christ; and he shall reign forever and
ever." "New Jerusalem shall come down
from God out of heaven"—"the tabernacle
of God is with men, and he will dwell with
them, and they shall be his people, and God
himself shall be with them, and be their God."
"Eye hath not seen, nor ear heard, neither
have entered into the heart of man, the things
which God hath prepared for them that love
him." "It doth not yet appear what we shall
be: but we know that, when he shall appear, we
shall be like him; for we shall see him as he is."

> "O'er the gloomy hills of darkness
>   Look, my soul, be still and gaze;
>   All the promises do travail
>   With a glorious day of grace."

Are there, indeed, no visible proofs in the
current history of our race that the world, in

spite of all the powers of darkness, is really advancing in all wisdom, grace, and goodness? Are there there no indications that the doctrines of heavenly truth are pervading the nations and leavening the whole world? If the promises are being fulfilled, the signs of fulfilment will not be wanting. Even a cursory survey of the Christian world does not fail to present to the appreciative eye most gratifying tokens of moral progress. If outward and visible fruits are to be taken as any indication of the inward and spiritual state, the present age has no cause to shrink from comparison with any of its predecessors. In all those charities which are the offspring of genuine benevolence and the exhibitions of that self-sacrificing love of our neighbor which Christianity alone inspires, no age of the world has surpassed or even equaled the present. Large sums of both public and private funds are annually expended in the erection and maintenance of hospitals for the relief of the afflicted poor. Comfortably housed and tenderly nursed, thousands of the poor are soothed in spirit and healed of disease by the kindly ministry of sympathizing Christians. Everywhere over the ever-widening domain of Christian civilization asylums, built and sustained at a cost of millions of money, stand as monuments of the liberality of Christians in providing for the relief and comfort of the insane, the blind, the deaf and dumb, and the orphan. Hundreds of thousands of dollars are annually expended in the publication and gratuitous distribution of religious literature with the sole view of extending the Redeemer's kingdom, while a number of societies organized for the especial purpose of printing and circulating the Bible are flooding the nations with the Word of God. In the establishment and endowment of schools and colleges increasing millions are every year bestowed in pure good will to men. Churches are being erected in the United States alone with such rapidity that each revolution of the earth presents complete and dedicated to God more than one on which the sun never shone before. These represent contributions of millions of dollars to the cause of God. In this country alone not less than sixty thousand men are exclusively engaged in preaching the gospel, supported at an annual expense of not less than thirty millions of dollars.

The Sunday-school has grown to be a mighty power, and, though using less money than many other agencies, accomplishes an amount of good which is incalculable. Without a dollar paid for salaries she employs more than a million of teachers and instruct many millions of children and older people, and furnishes for their reading a great variety of excellent literature. Perhaps no agency bestows so much labor without monetary consideration as the Sunday-school.

Missionaries have gone into all the world, and, armed with the sword of the Spirit, are pressing the battle against ignorance and sin. They have only to be supported by the prayers and the money of Christendom, and we shall see the heathen become Christ's inheritance and the uttermost parts of the earth his possession. Murders, lynchings, and other horrible crimes, still prevalent in Christian lands, do but indicate the intensification of the conflict between good and evil. Devils protested against the personal presence and power of Christ, and are still most signally manifest where the powers of good are strongest. Christ subdued and cast them out, and his word and Spirit shall still prevail to the final exorcism of devils from the hearts of men.

The missionary operations of the Christian world are so extensive and rapidly increasing that it is quite impossible to estimate their annual expenditures or achievements. Surely not less than 5,000 foreign missionaries are in the employ of the various branches of the Protestant Church in the world, exclusive of more than 10,000 native teachers and helpers in the different fields, who are supported at a yearly outlay of not much under $10,000,-000.

Of private and unrecorded Christian charities, known only to the giver, the receiver, and to God, eternity alone may reveal the uncounted millions bestowed and the blessed fruits which they will have produced. Such are a few of the more obvious and easily estimated, but by no means the highest, evidences of the progress of Christianity. Though founded on a basis of numerical and pecuniary calculation, they are none the less certain and satisfactory indications of the hold which religion has taken upon the hearts and purses of mankind, and are all the better adapted to this age when "money answereth all things" and even piety is most effectually expressed and most readily estimated by a pecuniary standard. These results show what is in men's hearts. The above-stated estimates show, too, not only the present state, but the rapid growth of Christianity, since the quantities they represent have increased tenfold in the last hundred years and fivefold at least in the last half-century. Can any, in view of these facts, suppose for a moment that real love of God and man is waning in the earth? Nay, the kingdom which was at first as a mustard-seed is spreading in spite of all opposition in many hearts and among all nations. It will fill the whole earth. The winding stream may in places seem to be flowing back toward its source, yet its real course is ever forward. So the onward march of Christ's kingdom may be checked or delayed, but is never reversed. Each age doubtless has its predominant vices, yet each has also its prevailing virtues, and virtue is ever the stronger in the end.

Then, friend, if your heart be in heaviness through manifold temptations, if the present look not so fair as the historic pictures of the past, if present experiences be not so happy as the sweet remembrances of youth, if the signs of promise be hid for a time from your eyes, spread not the veil of your despondency over the hopeful visions of the generations that are to follow you. Let not son or daughter hear words of faithless despondency from you. Blight not the energizing hopes of youth by distorted and embittered views of life. God's bow has not yet failed from the clouds, nor have the blessings of which it is

12

the pledge been withheld or diminished. If your increasing meetness for heaven lessen your appreciation of earthly good, take not away the signs of promise and the grounds of hope from those who are engaged in the mighty struggle to restore all things unto the heavenly pattern. "Say not, What is the cause that the former days were better than these? for thou dost not inquire wisely concerning this."

IF WE KNEW EACH OTHER BETTER.

Our frail and erring brother
    Is much the same as we,
And oft his hard surroundings
    Have made him what we see.
Perhaps he sees our failings,
    And counts them by the score.
If we knew each other better,
    We would love each other more.

Could we know his cranial structure,
    And feel his nervous strain,
The divinely fixed machinery
    Of hereditary brain.
We'd feel a thrill of mercy
    We never felt before;
When we know our brother better,
    We shall love our brother more.

When malice, hate, and vengeance
    Enrage the souls of men,
How nation against nation
    Hurls murderous missiles then!
Then ignorance of our brother
    Floods land and sea with gore;
When we know our neighbor better,
    We shall fight and slay no more.

North and South knew not each other
   Nor what they fought about;
Each saw the devil in his brother
   And thought to knock him out.
The devil's transmigrated,
   And laughed to see men fall;
Had these brethren known each other,
   They had never fought at all.

MONEY.

FEW subjects connected with human history are of more curious interest than that of money. Before discussing the dollar, which is our specific form of money, let us inquire somewhat into the nature, history, and functions of money in general.

The word "money" is derived from the Latin *Moneta*, a surname of Juno, in whose temple at Rome money was coined. Money is historically anything used in trade as a substitute for commodities. Men everywhere and always desire to exchange the products of their own labor for those of others. When one product is exchanged directly for another product the transaction is called barter. This method of exchange being found in many instances inconvenient or impracticable, men in all nations, from the earliest times, learned to employ substitutes for commodities, to avoid the cumbersomeness of exchange in kind. Different things have been used in different ages and countries for this purpose. The American Indians used wampum, or shells strung and woven into belts and neck-laces, some being white, the real wampum, and others dark or black. Our forefathers used leaden bullets; others have used nails, rings of copper, quills of salt or of gold-dust, shovel blades, and many other things, all of which seemed to possess some intrinsic value either for use or ornament. Lycurgus used iron for money in order to discourage extravagance among his people, although silver and gold had long been in use in buying and selling. He believed that so coarse and heavy a metal as iron could not be handled in sufficient quantities to purchase many luxuries. The Romans used sheep and cattle as media of exchange, hence our word "pecuniary," from the Latin *pecus*, a "herd."

While an indefinite variety of things have been made to serve the place of money, gold and silver were certainly among the earliest and have been by far the most extensively employed as money. Every civilized nation now uses them, and few, if any, barbarous ones are without them. Perhaps the first recorded instance of sale and purchase for money is that of Abraham buying a piece of ground for a burying-place, and weighing out the silver to pay for it.

Money may be defined as that which at any time and place all men agree to take in exchange for whatever they have to sell. It is virtually an order, endorsed by mankind, and of universal acceptance for every transferable power and possession of man. While many exchanges are made in kind and many commercial transactions are made by checks, orders, and other substitutes for money, yet none of these can supersede the necessity for the precious metals in the business of the world as a means of final payment. Money is to commerce what tools are to mechanical operations. Saws and hammers are scarcely more indispensable to the mechanic than is money in some form to the tradesman.

Why any particular thing should be adopted to represent all others is a very interesting question, which takes specific form when we inquire why silver and gold have been so universally adopted for this purpose, and are therefore called the precious metals. We know that neither of these metals is so useful as iron, yet each of them is many times more valuable in men's estimation. Their values arise largely from their use as money, as may be seen in the case of silver when its disuse for that purpose is threatened. For physical reasons it is very desirable that whatever is to measure all other values should itself possess much value in small compass. Money is not only exceedingly useful when exchanged for other things, but its terms and values are almost indispensable in measuring the values of articles to be exchanged in kind. One might be no little perplexed in exchanging horses of different qualities for land of varying fertility, unless he had some common measure of value to apply to each. Twenty-five horses, averaged at a value of sixty dollars each, would purchase one hundred acres of land averaged at fifteen dollars an acre. None but ideal dollars enter into this transaction, but he who fails to note that the ideal dollar is of very great importance has no adequate ideas on the subject of money.

As one of the chief functions of money is to measure and to transfer values, it may be well to define value, and especially to distinguish it from utility, with which many confound it. They are by no means the same, nor are they in proportion to each other in cases where they coexist. Many useful things have no value, and some valuable things have little utility. Air is useful, but not valuable, while diamonds have high value but are of little use. Value is simply purchasing power. Perry says: "Value is the relation of mutual purchase established between two commodities by their exchange."

Money is a representive of all values, and may be said to hold them in imperishable form. The value of the muscular power in a laborer's arm at any given moment, if not then exerted, is lost forever, while the shekels that Abraham paid his servants for a day's labor would command a day's labor still, if they were now in hand. One dollar may be made to pay a million of dollars of debts, if it be used often enough.

How does money originate? Is it a discovery or an invention, or is it the creature of the government, a thing that lives by statute law? Here we have a very broad and intricate question, which we shall not fully discuss. It is enough for our present purpose to say that the general agreement of mankind from immemorial time to use silver and gold as money, giving and receiving them in exchange for all transferable values, seems almost to demonstrate a providential design that they should be so used. It should not be overlooked that each of these metals has a value which is entirely independent of its use as money. Both would be extensively used if they were never coined as money. Just what part of their present values is due to the fact that they are used as money is an interesting question which it would be impossible to answer.

One of the most important inquiries connected with this whole matter of money is whether it is best to use one metal or two as money; and if two, what should be the relative values of the two. The world is now mightily exercised on these questions, and very much of the stability of commerce and of the prosperity of nations depends upon their proper solution. An able writer has said: " In its theoretic or economic respects money presents a field of apparently hopeless discord, controversy, and confusion, without a single doctrine established as a principle of universal or even of general acceptance." Some think that this is a question to be decided solely by legislation. They think that the government has power to create money, and that it should simply declare its will and settle the matter forever.

Doubtless the functions of government are of the highest importance in connection with this great question, but no government can

create money. Congress may do much to regulate currency, but it can not make money.
If Congress should authorize the stamping of
oak chips or leather buttons as money, would
that make them money? If the government
should stamp a piece of silver of the size of our
dime with the words, *one dollar*, would it pass
for one dollar? And could Congress make such
money a legal tender if it should try? Nations may weigh and stamp or coin gold and
silver, metals already in use, as money, but
no nation on earth has the power to endow
any metal or other material with the functions of money at its pleasure. As a matter
of fact, every nation in the world uses gold
for its chief currency, except Bolivia, Peru,
and a few of the smaller South American
republics; while every nation uses silver for
coins of smaller value. Silver is too bulky
and heavy to be handled in large amounts;
gold is far more convenient, and therefore
passes at about the same value among all
nations. A Mexican gold dollar is worth
about a dollar in the United States, but a Mex-

ican silver dollar passes for less than seventy-five cents, though it contains more pure silver than our dollar. This arises from the fact that silver bullion has fallen in the markets of the world, and our silver dollar is held above its real value by law.

The relative values of silver and gold have varied in past ages, as the following table will show; gold rising from nine to sixteen times the value of an equal weight of silver.

RATIO OF VALUE OF SILVER TO GOLD.

At Rome about the Christian era,				1 to	9
In England, mint price A.D. 1344,				1 "	12.475
"	"	"	1509,	1 "	11.400
"	"	"	1600,	1 "	11.100
"	"	"	1717,	1 "	15.209
"	"	"	1816,	1 "	15.209
"	"	"	1863,	1 "	15.069
In America		1893,		1 "	16

Gold. Silver.

Relative production in 1800 in ounces,	1 to	42
"	"	1863	"	1 "	63

In London during a crisis in 1847 no gold at all could be raised on £60,000 of silver; during a similar crisis in Calcutta in 1864 it was impossible to raise a single rupee of silver on £20,000 of gold, gold not being a legal tender. In recent days silver bullion has depreciated in the markets of the world till it can be bought for a little more than half its former price.

Whatever may constitute a currency, it is of the utmost practical importance that it be uniform and not fluctuating in quantity nor in value. It is the duty of the government to coin money in order to secure a uniformity in size and purity of coins and to prevent frauds. If two metals are used as currency, a great difficulty arises in keeping them at par with each other; indeed, it would be best to have the kind of currency in which a debt is to be paid specified in the contract. In the marts of trade dollars of different values would destroy confidence and obstruct commerce, and would be as the divers weights and divers balances which are declared by Solomon to be an abomination to the Lord. Those values which are to measure all other values should fluctuate as little as possible.

If money is appreciating in value, the creditor class are growing rich at the expense of the debtor; if money is depreciating, the debtor class is growing rich at the expense of the creditor. If two grades of money are in use at the same time, the inferior will invariably drive out the superior, since every one will buy goods and pay debts with the cheapest money that will pass. The government does not confer value upon money, but its power to decide what shall be legal tender may enable it to float unworthy money for a time. Should the government make other than real values a legal tender for debts, it would simply outrage and rob the people and stop all trade. All values grow out of the desires of men, and no law can create or increase men's desires. The government can give neither value nor price to commodities, and money is not an exception to this rule. Fiat money would prove to be a fraudulent delusion and practical impossibility. To authorize the payment for debts in it would be equivalent to the confiscation of property; to receive it in payment of taxes would speedily bankrupt the government. Governments adopt money which existed before they did. No government now in existence is as old as the purchasing power of gold and silver.

The unit of the money of the United States is the dollar. The word is of German origin, *thaler*, the coins having been first struck off in St. Joachim's valley or *thal*, in about the year 1518. It is not accurate to say that one hundred cents make a dollar; rather we should say that one dollar contains a hundred cents. The dollar is the unit, existing first in fact and in thought, and cents are fractions of it. Our silver dollar contains 371.25 grains of pure silver and 41.25 grains of alloy, making it weigh 412.5 grains. Our gold dollar contains 23.22 grains of gold and 2.58 grains of alloy, making it weigh 25.8 grains, ninetenths pure gold. English coined gold is $\frac{11}{12}$ pure and their silver $\frac{37}{40}$ pure. Previous to 1834 our gold coins contained 27 grains of gold to the dollar. The gold dollar is too small for convenient use, and is no longer coined. Our silver dollar was first coined about the year 1790. The pound sterling, or easterling as from the east, was originally and up to 1300 A.D. a pound Troy of silver, 11 ounces and 2 pennyweights pure and 18 pennyweights alloy. So the pound of money was a pound in weight. Now the pound in weight of silver makes 3£ 6s. of sterling money in the British Empire.

It is a common delusion with writers on money that the labor required to produce it is the source of its value. An encyclopedia says that "money has value put into it by costing labor and skill in bringing it into existence." This is an error. It is true that value is often in proportion to the cost of production, but the bestowment of labor can not confer value. A man might spend a lifetime of labor in carving an image out of a mountain which would have no value when he had finished it; while another might, without any labor at all, pick up a diamond worth thousands of dollars. Value springs from human desire and fluctuates with supply and demand.

13

Nor is utility the same as value. Water and air are useful, but valueless, the supply is free. A thing does not sell because men bestow labor on it, but because men want it and can not get it without buying it.

The fact that a metal is used as money certainly adds much to its value, since it may thus gratify a greatly enlarged sphere of desires; and the more extensively and thoroughly a metal answers this purpose, the more desirable it becomes for currency. If no government has power to fix the value of either gold or silver as related to commodities in general, then certainly none has power to fix their values in relation to each other. For a government to propose to change all the silver that may be brought to its mints into dollars of a given value in relation to gold would be perilous indeed. It would be equivalent to an offer to raise the price of all the silver bullion in the world to a par with gold as a ratio fixed by itself. Now, if a government can arbitrarily fix one ratio, why not another? If the Congress should enact that an ounce of gold shall be worth one hundred ounces of silver, could it make it so? The truth is, that the government, as a coiner of money, has nothing to do with fixing its value, but simply guarantees quantity and quality, the weight and the fineness of coins. Trade alone fixes values or fluctuates them (for they are *never fixed*), and it is only in the marts of trade that governments are mighty factors in fixing values. In collecting and disbursing taxes they largely influence prices and values. But should a government receive for taxes anything not current as money in the commercial world, it would stultify itself and ruin its credit. Our government did not originate our money; it simply adopted the Spanish silver dollar then in circulation, ordered similar ones to be coined, and adopted gold and silver for currency, as other nations had done from time immortal.

How much currency a nation needs we will not now discuss. Most enlightened nations seem to prosper best when the currency is from fifteen to thirty dollars for every inhabitant. It must be borne in mind, however, that the amount of trade is by no means limited to the volume of the currency. A very large majority of the trade of the world is carried on by means of bank-notes, checks, drafts (representative money), exchange of commodities, and balancing of accounts. Money seems to be needed chiefly to pay balances in trade between nations or individuals.

While, as we have said, all nations use gold for coins of larger value, no nation can dispense with silver for smaller currency. There seems to be an almost natural adaptation between the size, weight, and value of a silver dollar and an ordinary day's work. Perhaps eight-tenths of the cash transactions of the world involve not more than the value of a dollar. For all these gold is wholly unsuitable. Silver is for several reasons the best currency for such trade. It is durable, bright, too bulky to hoard, and too heavy to carry on the person in large quantities, easily coined, and has a musical ring. It goes and proves itself current by running. It would be a curious thing to trace the movements of some silver dollars for a year or even for a month. Probably one often does more purchasing or paying in a year than a thousand dollars of gold. Is not gold a lazy king, who has of late been growing fat by lying still? When men can make a better interest by investing their gold than by hoarding it, they will use it.

Good and lasting security and sure and large profits promote investments and enliven trade. In general, a depreciating currency promotes trade, since no man wishes to hold that which is growing less in his hands; while an appreciating currency checks investments and restricts trade, since men naturally hold to that which will be worth more to-morrow than it is to-day, and avoid contracting debts which must be paid in a currency whose cost is constantly increasing. Hence, when money is rising (in value) times are hard; when it is falling, times are easy; if it is falling fast, money will be plenty and times flush. Gold is now too precious to constitute the best currency—that is, it has too much purchasing power, while silver has too little. If the two could be tied together, or every debt be made payable one-half in silver and the other in gold, each metal being estimated by its price in the open marts of the world, a happy medium of trade would probably be found.

Much has been written and much learned about political economy, while but little is taught in books or in schools about personal economy—that is, the management of one's own finances. Indeed, it is not exaggeration to say that there are men who know enough about political economy to manage the exchequer of a nation, who yet can not manage their own personal expenses so as to "make ends meet" at home.

If we except sin and disease, there are perhaps no greater causes of unhappiness among men than poverty and debt. How to avoid these is a question of prime importance. Let every youth be taught how to earn a dollar and how to keep it till he has earned another, and not to spend more than one of these till he has earned two more, and never to go in debt. This rule will prevent poverty and lead to any degree of pecuniary abundance. Very many seem never to have learned that the saving of money is simply the storing away of the fruits of one's labor for future use, which must be done if we would avoid dependence upon the uncertainties of daily wages. The making and saving of money is largely a habit, which all should form. Among the inspired laws for the guidance of human life there is an emphatic doctrine on this subject: "If any provide not for his own, and specially for those of his own house, he hath denied the faith, and is worse than an infidel."

Wide-spread, thorough, and profound investigations of the question of money, as to what should constitute the body or the basis of currency—whether one of the precious metals or both should be taken as the standard money, and what should be their relative values if both be adopted, have occupied the wisest financiers through the ages, and have been especially earnest throughout the financial world in recent years. The Congress of

the United States seems to have been almost
hopelessly perplexed by these difficult prob-
lems. Ye may we not hope that these labo-
ious inquiries and extensive disturbances in
the commercial world will soon result in the
adoption of the same money by all civilized
nations, so that the coins of all, silver and
gold, shall circulate everywhere without dis-
count, estimated by their weight and fineness
alone? And will not such unity in the medium of trade have a powerful tendency to
unify the nations in spirit? Nations inter-
locked in commercial and financial interests
can not afford to fight each other. If God
works morally through men, and men work
chiefly through money, then it is through
money at last that God will transform the
world. When the money power of the world
shall have become subservient to Christ's
kingdom, then shall the "knowledge of the
Lord" speedily "cover the earth as the waters
cover the sea."

A scientific journal recently asked: What
invention is most needed now to advance the

civilization of the world? The answer given by one was: "A machine for storing without appreciable loss the electrical force generated by waterfalls, streams, tides, and other great natural dynamic agents."

Have we not just such an agency for storing and holding and transmitting to any desired distance, and applying in any desired way, the physical, intellectual, and even the moral forces of the world? Is there any known limit to the power of money? It supports thrones, equips and moves armies, measures the powers of nations and the extent of their dominions, fires brains, prints and distributes books, sends the heralds of the cross with the gospel to the heathen, and transforms the world by the ubiquity of its presence and the exhaustless applicabilities of its power. No seasons obstruct its movements, no climate affects its health, no dangers daunt its purpose. Epidemics do not alarm it, contagions do not infect it, and quarantines do not exclude it. It is everywhere welcomed, whether it come from friend or foe. It is the concentrated embodiment of the magnipotence of man. It is the efficient agent in every human achievement, but its most admirable form of work is in the realization of the benevolent purposes of God and man. This is preeminently the age of benevolence, when money, the embodiment of every form of power, is being employed as never before to conquer the forces of evil, and give universal reign to truth and righteousness.

Money not only builds railroads, digs canals, sends steamships across the ocean, and spans continents with telegraph wires and the ocean with submarine cables, but it illuminates the world with the light of electricity and with the light of the Word of God.

How wonderful is the fact that money loses none of itself in effecting its immeasurable achievements! The identical silver and gold which wrought their miracle as money and as plate in the erection and ornamentation of Solomon's temple may in our day be mightily aiding to bring to pass the far greater miracle of extending Christ's kingdom to the uttermost parts of the earth.

Money is indeed a thing of Protean forms, and undergoes its changes with marvelous facility. If money be put into a railroad, from the railroad money comes. If money feeds intellect, intellect reproduces money. It is transformed, but not lost. It is not only transformable and transmissible, but like a spirit may pass into different bodies, assume different shapes, and be transmitted to any place with ease. A bank draft weighing less than one-sixteenth of an ounce may move whole tons of silver or of gold.

Every power of man's body and of man's soul may find its most efficient expression through the agency of money.

AUTUMN.

I.

A RURAL SCENE.

Since 'tis meet the ripening year
Should in richer robes appear;
Autumn's dress takes gorgeous hues
From the sunshine and the dews.
While with chemic rays the sun
Dyes the leaflets one by one,
Fields and forests gleam and glow,
One vast panoramic show.
Poplars clad in green and gold,
Towering tops like banners hold;
Sweetgums shine in fiery red,
The oak too lifts its blazing head.
See vast forests far and near,
Changing with the changing year.
Fields display more brilliant flowers
Than were theirs in vernal hours:
Swaying ranks of goldenrod,
Lengthening plumes conspicuous nod;
Seas of floral beauties glow
With more tints than painters know,
While the varying shades declare
Hand divine paints everywhere—
Hues that angels might admire
Wonder, love, and joy inspire.

Strolling through these woodland wilds,
Rapture every sense beguiles.
Shadows from the sylvan height

Broider far the fields of light,
Awe pervades the slumbrous air,
Glory lingers everywhere,
Silence reigns o'erhushing all,
Does she hear the leaflets fall?
O how sad, so fair a scene
May to-morrow but have been!
For when south wind moistly blows,
Every leaf its breathing knows;
Won by its mysterious wooing
Hence ere long they all are going,
Quitting these enchanting bowers,
Quivering down in golden showers.
Late in autumn's frosty days
Pale wich-hazel's leafless sprays
From their unpretentious bloom
Send a rare and rich perfume
Till the air with fragrance laden
Soothes like odors fresh from Eden.
Here I linger hours away,
Here forget the passing day.
Ah! could mortal skill redeem
Aught from time's resistless stream
These blest days would I dissever,
And would make them mine forever.

II.

BIRDS IN AUTUMN.

Once in early autumn days,
So the beech-tree legend says,
Robin Redbreast's youngest son
Died when life had just begun.
Lost by chance from mother's nest,
Fate denied him other rest.
Downy drapery dipped in dew

Chilled the birdling ere he flew.
Father drooped upon the tree,
Mother mourned in minor key,
Birds around in sadness pine,
Dimly too the sun did shine,
Falling leaves dropped slowly down,
Sounds were sad, the earth grew brown,
Winds sang dirges in the air,
Gloom was brooding everywhere.
Sad and rueful was the day
When young Robin passed away.
Curling leaf was shroud and grave,
Drooping branch did o'er him wave.
Silence reigned long time they say,
On young Robin's burial day.

Yet the sadness soon was past,
Sorrow but a night did last,
Sharpest grief takes quickest flight,
Songs came with the morning light;
Joy thrilled all the birds again—
Joy is stronger after pain.
Hear the mock-bird's autumn lays,
Mellow as the autumn days.
Day and night I hear him sing,
Fresh as in the burst of spring.
Now, too, hear the flute-toned wren,
Calling o'er and o'er again,
Till the silvery notes deploy
Flinging wide the sounding joy.
List! the speckle-breasted thrush,
Creeping through the tangled brush,
Chatters threats, with baneful eye,
At the heedless passer-by.

Now the birds with prudent care
Store away their winter fare,

For they all appear to feel,
While yet distant, coming ill,
And prepare for it betimes,
Or depart to friendlier climes.
Nature, too, makes them to know
Which should stay and which should go.

Sporting now in airy ocean,
Swallows whirled in wild commotion,
Congregate at evening hour,
Down some chimney-throat to pour.
Moved by strangest inspiration,
They prepare for their migration;
Seeming every one to know
Just the time for them to go.
Thousands upon thousands come,
Gathering for their journey home.
Bluebirds, too, go southward now,
Till the time when farmers plow;
Man may hear their concert chime,
When they start for distant clime.

Marshaled high in pathless skies,
Bird to wandering bird replies;
Plaintive notes borne through the air,
As of angel near despair,
Heard amid our dreamy slumbers,
Wake us by their mystic numbers,
Marking tardy hours of night
Slowly passed in weary flight—
Signal-sounds on high to tell
Heaven and earth that all is well.

III.

THE FALLING OF THE LEAVES.

One by one they lose their hold;
Some are crimson, some are gold,

Some are pied and some are brown—
All come circling gently down.
Quitting shrub and lofty tree,
Giddy things the leaves must be.
Wafted through the airy ocean,
Whirling all in glad commotion,
Swaying oft with unheard sound,
Veering coyly to the ground.

Trembling on the plain below,
Kissing breezes o'er them blow,
Soothing the vast company
With low, rustling harmony.
Fading each without a sigh,
Cheery deaths the leaves must die!

Covering o'er the hills and dales,
Tiny plants from frosty gales:
Comfort they to others give,
Die that other leaves may live,
Beautify the mourning earth,
Give to future glorious birth.

In autumnal splendors clad,
Their departing is not sad;
They gave spring and summer grace,
They give charm to autumn's face.

Falling from their stations high,
Monarchs' crowns beneath us lie;
Realms bereft and kings made bare,
Yield the tints that mingle here.
Mansion hall was never spread
With such carpet as we tread,
When the earth herself adorns
With the gifts of all her sons.

www.ingramcontent.com/pod-product-compliance
Lightning Source LLC
Chambersburg PA
CBHW020619030726
47497CB00007B/2315